OSHO
THE FIRST BUDDHA IN THE DENTAL CHAIR

Amusing Anecdotes By His Personal Dentist
SWAMI DEVAGEET

Copyright ©2013
Sammasati Publishing and Devageet Newman
First American Edition 2013
Library of Congress Control Number: 2013934471

ISBN#: 9780615632230 (hardcover)
Sammasati Trade Catalog Number: SA1117

Published by: Sammasati Publishing
Art Director: Waduda Paradiso
Edited by: Mallika Magner
Design and Layout by: Nikesha Breeze
Photos by: Seema Venizelos
Executive Producer: Bhikkhu Schober

All rights reserved. No part of this document may be reproduced or transmitted in any form or by any means, electronic, mechanical, photocopying, recording, or otherwise, without prior written permission of Company Name.

Printed and bound in China

Sammasati
publishing

Sammasati Publishing
PO Box 20081
Boulder, CO 80308
www.sammasatipublishing.com

Boulder Inats 2013

To George and Sedena
.... where are woods
met .... here now
always ♡
love Walhle

hope you enjoy!
P Bhikkhu

This book is dedicated to Osho who describes his life on Earth as a visit to this planet. For Osho life itself is god. Gratitude is too small a word to describe the magnitude of change that his presence continues to bring into my life.

Swami Devageet. 2012. Edinburgh.

Table of Contents

Acknowledgements	XI
Author's Note:	XII
Bhagwan to Osho	XV
An Ancient Meditator Reflects On His Master; Osho	22
The First Time	37
Sheela's Misplaced Effort	58
Love and Dentistry	62
Only Skidding	70
Wading for the First Appointment	81
Becoming Osho's Notetaker	93
The Master's Alchemical Surgery	108
My Days Were Numbered	131
Golden Glimpses	138
The Fearful Specialist	144
"You can kill me but do not harm my moustache ..."	159
Closure Osho Style	168
The Ear, The Tooth, and Beyond	184
Osho's Akashic Transmission:	202
Almost Meeting A Remarkable Man	223
Dental Fire Test: Are You My Dentist Or My Disciple?	232
The Last Golden Glimpse	249
The Life of Osho | *a Timeline*	261

Acknowledgements

I am deeply grateful to Bhikkhu and Waduda of Sammasati Publications, Santa Fe, for creating their publishing company for the express purpose of bringing the authentic truth of Osho to a wider public, authentic truth as experienced by the few who lived in his close proximity.

I want to thank my editor, Mallika Magner, whose enthusiasm and zest for the project supported my lack of confidence in myself as a writer. She told me that editing this book has brought her to a new, deeper understanding of Osho. I enjoyed working with her alongside.

For my beloved, Kamala, thanks are not enough to describe her support, love and unfailing trust that Existence will find a publisher for this book. She is an unfailing source of inspiration, and, she was right.

And of course, I wish to thank Ma Prem Ashu, and Ma Prem Nityamo. As Osho's chairside dental assistants, they participated in many of the events described. Ours was a rare and wonderful partnership. I thank them for being such great company.

Swami Devageet. Edinburgh. December 2012.

Author's Note:

While on his 'world tour' Osho had sent word from his unknown whereabouts (later found to be Portugal) asking me to write a book detailing my life with him, to be entitled: Bhagwan, Messiah of Life, Love and Laughter: a subjective account of my life with the enlightened master, Bhagwan. He changed his name to Osho in 1989, and I later changed the title accordingly.

Osho The First Buddha in the Dental Chair: Amusing Anecdotes By His Personal Dentist, is the second book he asked me to write, in 1987. These dental anecdotes focus mainly on events, giving only a minimal background sketch of their historical context.

Osho: Messiah of Life, Love and Laughter, has a different focus. It follows the timeline from my first meeting with Bhagwan, to when he left his body as Osho. It contains details of time, place, people and situations, which provide an understanding of the background context for the events being described. It details three main phases of my life with Osho; the first, as a sannyasin in the early days of the Ashram in Pune; the second, in Rajneeshpuram, Oregon, USA.; the third, Pune from 1987 until January 19, 1990, when he left his physical body. This book will offer future generations with a detailed, hands-on, personalized view of those tumultuous, rapturous days.

Writing these books is a gift, and also a responsibility. Future readers will come to know Osho through these pages. I have trusted my own experience of Osho. His words, especially in the dental room are as I remember them. He trusted me to remember. In Chapter 14, I describe an "Akashic Transmission," no other words fit what transpired: reading it you will understand. I had asked, at the time, if I should take notes while he spoke. He told me there was no need, that I would remember. I have remembered. In this book his words, as I remember them, are in italics.

I hope the errors in style due to my lack of literary skills are more than compensated by the unique vantage point I offer from having been in the lion's mouth.

BHAGWAN TO OSHO

BHAGWAN SHREE RAJNEESH was a name used by the man who later chose to become known as Osho. 'Bhagwan' is a title given in India to individuals recognized as having reached the highest peaks of spiritual consciousness. Previously he had been known as 'Acharya Rajneesh'. 'Acharya' means 'spiritual teacher.'

In his Acharya days he was a young firebrand endlessly touring India, debating, challenging and arguing with the finest minds – intellectual, spiritual and political – of his time. As an undergraduate he had won the prestigious All-India University Students Debating Championship. Enlightenment came to him at the age of twenty-one.

After his enlightenment he completed a doctorate in philosophy, gaining the annual gold medal as the University of Jabalpur's most brilliant graduate. He threw the medal down a well, in an act symbolizing his rejection of the trap of respectability.

Later, as a young professor of philosophy, his already impressive dialectical skills broadened with his enlightenment into a whole new dimension. He became feared and respected, in equal measure. Those in high office whom he challenged in debate feared to encounter his intellect and passion. Simultaneously, as a result, he was becoming increasingly acclaimed by India's considerable intelligentsia as a new force, a powerful voice to be reckoned with. As his spiritual wisdom and fearsome clarity became even more widely known, Acharya Rajneesh was increasingly referred to as 'Bhagwan,' 'The Blessed One.'

As Bhagwan Shree Rajneesh, he was known worldwide to hundreds of thousands of people for his spiritual presence, his wit, wisdom and charisma. He was a seer who riled the rulers, provoked the pompous and challenged the intelligentsia to take a wide look at where they are leading humanity. Although an archetypal sage, a fount of human wisdom, he remained a spontaneous, immensely lovable person in whom full-spectrum intelligence and erudition lived happily in rare neighborliness with raw humour. The man, now known as Osho, brought these unlikely elements together allowing his inner alchemy to transmute them into uniquely effective tools for the transformation of human consciousness.

"A sane man in an insane world looks mad" he would say, in response to media reports that tried to make sense of a tourist in the US who apparently owned ninety-three Rolls Royces, most of which he never drove. In the US, a nation whose religious fervor is reserved almost entirely for a long-dead, poor, Jewish mystic who famously rode on a donkey, Osho's ironic opulence was as difficult to swallow as his startlingly obvious spirituality.

The western world prefers their spiritual leaders to be safely dead. Their message can then be happily twisted into whatever shape fits the current comfort zone. Osho was alive, too alive, spontaneous and unpredictable, for those whose beliefs have petrified their spirit, and paralyzed their quest for living truth. That Osho loved the game of life is evident in his style. He played it magnificently, with gusto and elan. Changing his name was part of the game. After all, a rose by any other name is still a rose.

In the last months of his physical life Osho changed his name not just once but several times. He wrote his own epitaph: Never born, never died, visited this planet between December 12, 1931, and January 19, 1990.

Some people have re-invented themselves: Osho de-invented himself. His name cycle began when he declared that he was rejecting the name "Bhagwan," and taking, instead, the new appellation, "Our Beloved Master." He asked for all of his six hundred and forty books to be changed accordingly. His publishers, with much hand-wringing, struggled to accomplish their task.

In characteristic fashion, in a morning discourse during this phase, he told his audience of many hundreds, that he had never liked to be called "Bhagwan," and had only tolerated it because he did not want to upset his many Indian sannyasins who, according to ancient Hindu tradition, considered "Bhagwan" to be a recognition of the blessings they see apparent in a man at the peak of human spiritual attainment. All Buddhas in India, he explained, have been named "Bhagwan" – The Blessed One. *"But,"* he said, in Hindi, *"the word 'Bhag' means* cow's vagina. And because Hindus revere the cow as the holy mother of humanity they think the name 'Bhagwan' is supremely holy. But I am not Hindu, and I have never liked to be named after a cow's vagina, holy or not."

A little later, "Our Beloved Master" announced, following a dream by one of his devotees, that he was now to be known as, "Maitreya the Buddha." The dream had recognized Our Beloved Master to be the living incarnation of Gautama the Buddha. Buddhist scriptures state that Maitreya was the name given by Gautama the Buddha to his future incarnation. His long-suffering book publishers were asked to make the changes from 'Our Beloved Master' to 'Maitreya the Buddha.' As Maitreya the Buddha, he announced in his evening discourse that he had invited Gautama the Buddha to step out of two and a half millennia of timelessness and make his home in Lao Tzu House[1]. Not only that, but to also share the blood, bones and organs of a living Buddha. It was a gracious invitation of a mystical magnitude beyond the grasp of most sannyasins[2].

Although this was a unique union, never previously known, and almost certain to never be repeated, it was doomed from the start. The ancient spirit of Gautama the Buddha, according to the contemporary Maitreya the Buddha, was too fixated with his ancient austere spiritual practices to be happy living in modern luxury. The

---

1. Osho's personal house in his ashram
2. Name of Osho's disciples

contemporary wonders of bathroom hygiene and technology, especially the Jacuzzi, apparently freaked out Gautama and created intolerable friction between the old and the new. Maitreya the Buddha was thus obliged to request Gautama the Buddha to return to his timeless abode.

Soon after Gautama left Lao Tzu for the wider realms of Existence, inevitably, the name 'Maitreya the Buddha' was also dropped. The anguish of the book publishers who were still monumentally struggling to complete the massive change from "Bhagwan" to "Our Beloved Master," then to "Maitreya the Buddha," reached new peaks. Six hundred and forty books in various states of name-change were now in a nameless limbo, in resonance with their author's state of mystical namelessness. Not long afterwards this supremely mischievous mystic chose to be called Osho.

The name-game, played with such evident gusto by Osho, illustrates not only his sense of humour, it is also an example of how he created outrageous devices to challenge his sannyasins egos. Osho created a koan from the ancient question, "What's in a name?"

Osho is a man before his time, perhaps beyond time itself. As quantum reality melts away old notions separating time and space, Osho's impact on the human collective unconscious psyche may eventually seep into the zealously protected domains of the high and the mighty, challenging the great and the good. Osho regularly showed such people to be neither great, nor good, and that is probably why his name is rarely mentioned among the echelons of contemporary, western intelligentsia. Despite holding the Guinness Book of Records for the largest number of books by a single author, he is studiously ignored, neither mentioned in footnotes nor bibliographies, in studies on consciousness, religion, philosophy, mind-body healing or spiritual transformation. Yet in all of these fields he offers a masterly clarity that blows away the fog of false beliefs and empty theoretical speculation. His is the living truth of an authentic mystic, the experiential reality of being-as-consciousness. Osho's life shows how to actualize higher consciousness into daily reality. His vision opens new portals of human possibility.

But Osho remains too hot to handle even now, these many years after his physical death. The media endlessly and deliberately celebrates the froth of the false: it sells. They continue to mock or ignore the indomitable enlightened mystic who openly challenges the dark domains of power ruled by the priests and the politicians and the global corporations who hold a sleeping humanity by the throat.

Osho is a real man, a timeless exemplar of indomitable clarity and courage, whose vision raises the collective consciousness of humanity from darkness to light, individual by individual. In this book I hope to show Osho's vision in action by telling of those marvelous times when I was at the teeth of the master.

Devageet. November 27, 2012. Edinburgh.

Bhagwan to Osho

"My message is not a doctrine, not a philosophy. My message is a certain alchemy, a science of transformation."

Prologue
An Ancient Meditator Reflects On His Master: Osho

Now in the endgame, it is time to recollect the impact Osho has in my life. Meeting him has been the single, most significant event in a life full of events: an eve-of-war birth to working class Jewish parents in London; twice sent to foster parents as an infant to avoid wartime bombing; my father's severe heart condition; my brother's birth and almost-simultaneous death from pneumonia; food rationing; grammar school and university in post-war England; an early marriage; the death of my father weeks after the birth of my first son; graduating as a dental surgeon; the births of three more children; becoming a passionate painter-dentist and moving the whole family to Australia; my mother's second marriage, and much more, all of which happened before I was thirty years old.

This life full of incident always had an undercurrent, a barely coherent thought that my life was lacking something, an unknown, vital ingredient. The sense of missing something of great significance burned in me like fire urging me to seek and search, but for what? I did not know, but the anguish of my inner ignorance was undeniable and constant.

I was in the middle of my life when I first met Osho

in 1976. In that moment, the world as I knew it shifted on its axis. Words cannot fully convey the massive impact of first seeing him. It was not simply the effect of his astonishing beauty and grace, but in that single moment I recognized him as the person I had been unknowingly searching for.

It was an immense, wonderful inner shock accompanied by a tidal wave of sheer elation, a blast of exhilaration that tore through me as I saw him emerge through the plain painted doorway in Chuang-Tzu Auditorium in his ashram in Pune. Simultaneously came slow-falling tears of healing and a marvelous sense of inner release. The very sight of Osho brought an interior explosion that goes on even now, thirty-six years later.

The timing of meeting my master was exactly right. My life props were falling away: my marriage, and with it my home, family and professional life in a small town; a five-year course on oriental philosophy was complete. My passion for painting faded once I put my fire into what I thought was meditation.

The fire in my belly urged me to keep looking, but the new ideas and concepts that I found only added more mental furniture to an already overburdened mind. I was stuffing my head full while my heart was yearning for inner space.

That explosively singular moment of first seeing Osho shifted my mode of consciousness from searching to finding. In that instant of recognition I knew that I had found what I never really thought possible, a guiding light that irrevocably pierced to the very centre of my being. I felt that I had come home at last.

I met him on April 6, 1976. The world was different then. I too was very different, unrecognizable to my eyes now.

When I first arrived in Pune I only knew of Osho's vision from two of his books: "The Way of The White Cloud," and "No Water, No Moon." [1] His words were clear and brilliant, but when I heard him speaking, the unique quality of his voice lifted me into another, altogether unknown and ineffable region. I felt the consciousness carrying his words singing a silent melody that breathed new life into my heart. For me, hearing Osho giving his daily discourse was like hearing a long-lost love song that touched my heart and awakened my soul.

On becoming initiated into sannyas that same month, Osho gave me the name 'Swami Devageet.' *"It means Divine Harmony. Swami means seeker of the eternal, and Devageet means the Divine Song of Existence...."*

As a sannyasin, the effect of his words was further enhanced. Daily, his discourses pulled me into the timeless harmony of their source. I bathed in the cool, fresh waters of my own inner freedom that began to flow as I thankfully allowed my English repressions and inherited Jewish beliefs – uneasy bedfellows from the beginning – to be

---

Published by Osho International www.osho.com

washed away by his living river of consciousness. Intense psychotherapy groups in the ashram supported the letting-go process initiated by Osho.

In these groups, I happily screamed, fought, laughed and emoted my way through my ancient repressions. Inhibitions fell by the wayside and I was carried high on the wave of energy that became available to me. The therapists were sannyasins, and, through them, I could feel Osho's presence encouraging me to open my ancient floodgates.

On my first visit to the ashram in Pune, I stayed for four weeks, and was continually astonished as my meditation gave me a direct experience of what I had only previously read. My first therapy group – the AUM Marathon – was startling: I experienced dimensions of consciousness completely unknown to me. I was so ripe that I popped open. In those four weeks I came alive in a completely new way. I wanted nothing more than to live and work forever in Osho's ashram.

I came to live in the Shree Rajneesh Ashram in Pune in December 1978. It had taken time and effort to finalize my divorce and settle my affairs.

Osho made it easier for me to cut the strings that bound me. During my leaving meeting with him on my first visit, I had told him of my impending divorce, telling him that I still loved my wife. I wanted to share with her the wonder I had found in his presence, but our advanced state of marital warfare had made any communication seem an aggressive act.

Looking at me thoughtfully he had said, *"You say nothing to her, just give her everything: the house, the money, the children, the furniture, the dental practice, the cars, the insurances. Keep nothing back. Then she will know that something has really happened for you here."*

Back in England I did as he instructed. My divorce lawyer thought I had lost my sanity in India. In reality the opposite had happened.

Arriving to work at the ashram in 1978, I was given the job of ashram dentist in the tiny newly-designed dental surgery. In 1979, I had been living in the ashram for one year when I was asked to be Osho's personal dentist. He told me, *"Gautama the Buddha had a personal physician, but no Buddha has ever had a disciple as his personal dentist; especially someone like you, Devageet. I am the first Buddha in the dentist's chair, but make no mistake, I may be in your dentist's chair but you are on my operating table!"*

In the years from 1968 until 1980, a window of new hope – Flower Power – opened briefly in the human collective psyche. Popular music led the way forward, opening the eyes and hearts for a whole newly-liberated youth generation, giving a voice to the angst and passion of the awakening youth movement who, confronted by the futile brutality of Vietnam, wanted to make love, not war.

What a time it was. A new era of freedom had suddenly emerged and the old bastions of authority were taken by surprise. Bras were burned, sexual inhibitions were blowing in the wind of change. Dope and hope filled the air. Freedom became the password to a new future. Old standards became irrelevant as a buoyant, confident, brash new counter-culture birthed itself.

A whole new generation, newly mobile and undeniably nubile, was swept along by the heady fervor and sensual delights unexpectedly and openly available. Inevitably, freedom showed itself to have two faces; freedom from, and freedom for. Mostly, they knew passionately what they wanted to be free from; few knew, or considered what to do with freedom when it happened. Freedom without responsibility, for many, soon became license. Hedonism beckoned irresistibly: on a clear day one could see forever. We thought, in that all-too-brief window of time, we could see the future, and it was us. We were the future as it was happening.

Osho's historical timing was impeccable. The newly – awoken generation loved his passionate, cool fire. They came, first in tens, then hundreds, then in thousands. We, the new generation, were pilgrims, whether we realized it or not, searching for a new, better way of living. On hearing Osho's clear call we came running from every walk of life.

We arrived in Pune as pilgrims thirsty for truth, emerging from a worldwide cultural wilderness that offered war in the name of peace, empty promises in place of true values, and old religious dogmas falsely claiming to be the road to salvation. In Osho we found something quite different: a fountainhead of clear truth brimming with love. Thousands came to drink at his well and I took care of their well-traveled teeth.

Osho's ashram in Pune offered the newly awakening generation something in addition to freedom. Not only freedom from past repressive cultural conditioning, but also, and most significantly, a powerfully attractive alternative. Osho envisioned a whole new humanity with a whole new consciousness, a future society whose values were based on authentic, individual spiritual experience in which life itself is God.

He made it clear that his vision starts with each individual being responsible for oneself and for the world, emphasizing that only meditation can guide the way from the darkness of the past to the direct personal experience of one's inner light of intrinsic reality. It is the inner light that illumines the way forward. He offered a radical, totally original spiritual path that included all the joy, juice and jubilation that enable a human being to celebrate being authentically human.

He touched the hearts, minds and souls of seekers from every nation, culture and religion, his clarity shone a probing light into the dark shadows of the worldly cynical hypocrisy of daily politics and religion, revealing how a dull, unwitting, sleepy humanity is being kept dumbed-down in order to be ruthlessly duped and manipulated by priests, politicians and global corporations into giving away their power, control, and money. Osho, with piercing erudition, and a rare, raw humor, exposed the sick minds hiding beneath the tawdry trappings of power.

Armed only with love, laughter, supreme wisdom, intelligence, and indomitable courage, this lone man from central India became, in the late twentieth century, a troubadour of the spirit whose shining eyes and infectious humour breathed new life into those souls in whom hope was still a vital ember.

He showed that none of the so-called emperors had any clothes, and like in the ancient story, it was the younger generation who first recognized the naked truth revealed by his vision. He reminded us that the powers that hold humanity in bondage are neither innocent nor accidental; they know their lies, and they hate to be exposed. He stripped away their strategies, exposed their motives and revealed the stink of corruption.

Faced by such a broad attack on their proven strategies, and seeing how many young, intelligent, highly-educated people were being attracted by this phenomenal man from India, several national governments – from the United States, UK, Australia, South Africa, Israel, and others – sent secret agents to investigate the impertinent challenger. Usually posing as journalists, agents came to scrutinize the man who dared to say what many thought but themselves lacked the courage and the clarity to express. Agents disguised as seekers came to criticize and to sneer at this gentle, smiling man, exotically and elegantly dressed, who brought complex worldly and spiritual issues into simple, clear words that reached out and touched those who could still listen.

Some journalists, who originally had come to belittle the younger generation's foolishness, stayed in the ashram in Pune, themselves becoming sannyasins; after all, who knew better than they the rank odor of corruption in the dark corridors of power described so eloquently by Osho.

Inevitably, the dogs guarding humanity's imprisoned splendor began to show their fangs. They sniffed danger from this lone individual in whose presence the impossible seemed not only to be possible, but probable. Whereas the old religions had made humanity appear senile and impotent, dependent on an ineffective priesthood for salvation, Osho lifted the human spirit into a new vitality. Most alarming of all was that he made his tremendous impact across the world seem effortless, even fun; and effortless effort is the hallmark of a true enlightened master. They smelled danger.

They covertly set in motion the unseen machinery of government to use the local and international media to counter the "Bhagwan effect." The yellow press in Pune regularly and predictably railed against sannyasins' "loose morals." The almost daily press attacks goaded local Hindu fundamentalists into violence: a would-be assassin threw a knife at Osho during a discourse. Police were watching as the knife was thrown, yet the resulting court case was thrown out due to "lack of evidence." That was the day of my first dental session with him.

Later, during Osho's medical emergency, when two of his lower back vertebrae collapsed, his secretary applied for a visa to America for possible spinal surgery. Negative press reports from India were used to justify the official obstacles placed in the way of his application. Long before he went to the United States he was regarded by officialdom as a dangerous individual based on the lies and prejudices of the yellow press of India. He knew the dangers he faced from the religious right in America, the famous Moral Majority, and its influence on their born-again president. When I first arrived in Madras, Oregon, in August 1981, weeks before his arrival, the local newspaper headline read, "Another Jonestown." It was evident that forces against Osho were being activated even before he came to Oregon. Osho showed no fear. Along with Nietzsche, he joyously declared, "God is dead," fearlessly announcing that the priests and politicians were leading mankind to global suicide. Osho did not mince his words of denunciation: *"I stand against the whole rotten past of humanity."*

The work of an enlightened master is strange, it has to be. *"In an insane world a sane man looks mad,"* is how he put it. His work is to liberate the mind of the disciple, to release their whole consciousness-as-being from the unconscious ego-self. To enable his work, Osho created many devices, each aimed to release the conditioned mind of the disciple from its invisible web of false identification derived from education, culture, religious beliefs, family attitudes, opinions, ideologies, "isms" of all kinds woven into a dense ego, a false self, an armor-plated pretender to the throne of consciousness that prevents direct contact with one's intrinsic, original wholeness. It is through this thick shell of unconsciousness that Osho's devices need to drill in order for individuals to regain their unknown, imprisoned splendor. Once the shell of unconsciousness is breached, awareness is liberated, and meditation can reach new depths of being.

"Your diseases may be many but my medicine is one: meditation, witnessing. It heals all your diseases, and all healing is a function of love."

Osho, as an enlightened master, one who has come to realize himself, not by following any religious tradition but by his own immense clarity, recovered his eternal, original wholeness of being, and speaks on his own authority. He repeatedly hammered the point that meditation is the only time-proven, safe way out of the maze of mental conditioning.

As the years have passed the word "meditation" has been marketed and branded into a parody of its original meaning. Thousand of meditation methods are now available, but meditation is not a technique, and they lay a false trail. The direct realization of intrinsic, pristine consciousness comes when awareness has sufficient clarity to recognize, and go beyond, mental activity. Meditation is consciousness in the state of inner witnessing, and as such it rises above the clouds of thoughts into the untouched, untouchable vastness of consciousness-as-being. Witnessing becomes the catalyst that pierces the false and reveals the true.

For most, the ego-personality-mind is the known, certain self. It may be more accurately regarded as a left-brain-hemisphere's notion of self. Western cultural values and education have a long tradition of deriding introspection, regarding information from the right-brain-hemisphere as unreliable, unprovable, mystical, vacuous and irrational, sniffily reduced to "mere navel-gazing." For left-brainers, meditation, if it exists at all, is nonsensical, suggesting a wooly-minded, anti-scientific vagueness. However, attitudes, along with the times, are a-changing.

The last years of the twentieth century saw science challenging its own orthodoxy. Driven by the supra-rational world of quantum reality, physics has been forced to let go its long-held Newtonian certainties. Uncertainty itself became a pillar of the new physics. The late twentieth century, saw meditation – a similar, supra-rational challenge to the limitations of rationality – emerging from its orphaned state into legitimacy. The science of consciousness has begun to emerge into its own light.

In the dental room Osho was the enlightened master at work. His words, gestures, and silent presence encouraged each person there to turn their attention inwards, to become aware of being aware.

From the dental chair, he provoked me to face my inner barriers. Stripping off my masks and facing my inner, unknown self was often arduous and uncomfortable. I consoled myself by seeing him in the role of a mother bird demonstrating the gift of flight by her own example, as he nudged me from my comfort zone to fly by myself, to find my own wings. In the unique intense intimacy of the dental room, face to face with Osho, it was impossible to hide. He was a dental mirror in which I could not avoid seeing my self.

He often took me to depths where my trust in him was the only light in my inner darkness. There I discovered the wisdom of a loving heart that opens the ancient doors leading from mind, to no-mind, into being. He showed me that awareness is the golden key, meditation the door, and the master is the living proof of his message.

I see now that Osho used the dental room to create a conscious work of objective art, a masterly drama in three acts: Pune before America; Osho in Oregon; and the endgame, Returning to Pune. The scenes for the drama, were mostly, but not all, set on the apparently mundane stage of dentistry. He created situations, devices, for each person present, but I can only legitimately speak of those that peeled my mind free from its past to reveal the sacred centre where being and consciousness merge into unity and wholeness. I can speak of his effect on me only now, these many years later, because the seeds he sowed took this time to germinate.

Osho was not just *a* dental patient, he was *the* dental patient, and what a patient! *"Devageet, you are obstinate, but I am more obstinate. I will not stop until I break open your concrete skull."*

In the annals of dentistry I guess that no dentist has ever heard such a statement from his dental chair.

In these anecdotes I have tried to describe Osho, the master, at work, on me, his personal dentist, and on humanity itself. Traditionally, disciples come to the feet of the master; for me, as existence danced its mystery, I found myself at the teeth of the master. A unique, wonderful experience, which, even now, thirty-six years later, continues unabated.

Devageet Miasto, ITALY, 2012.

Chapter 1
The First Time

Once, after a hypnotherapy group, in Osho's ashram in Pune, India in 1977, Osho asked me how it had been. I told him I had experienced real terror, and wonderful fantasies.

"*Which was real?*" he asked. I thought briefly before answering, "The fear was real. The fantasies were too good to be true."

> *"Can you see, Devageet, how mind rejects the beautiful and the good as unreal. It condemns them as mere imagination because they have never before happened to you. Yet that same mind never questions the reality of any negative experience. Your pain and your misery are never questioned; they are always accepted as real, utterly real.*
>
> *Why? Because mind is familiar with suffering; that is its reality. Mind never allows the truth of any positive experience. Mind is conditioned, trained by harsh experience, to only see reality in the negative. Your brain is a bio-computer programmed for your survival. It does not see truth. It is not concerned with truth. It functions*

only to keep your body alive. The brain is biological. Truth, beauty, bliss, love, joy and harmony ... they have no survival value as far as the mind is concerned, hence it dismisses them as unreal, valueless. Their truth can be seen only by the heart, not by the mind, and the mind goes on denying the realities of the heart as mere fantasy."

It was a sunny morning in 1977. I was breakfasting happily on bread and banana while sitting with Sagaro, my girlfriend, in the tranquility that follows Osho's morning discourse. It was our routine to sit on the Zen wall, outside Lao Tzu Gate, during the short time before our daily work began. I had been the ashram dentist since arriving at the Shri Rajneesh Ashram, in Pune, India, from London the year before. Sagaro worked with the team who handled all the ashram correspondence.

I had taken sannyas on April 9, 1976, three days after meeting Osho for the first time. Taking sannyas, becoming an Osho sannyasin, meant leaving my past behind and dedicating myself to a life of meditation and self-study and awareness.

Osho was called Bhagwan Shree Rajneesh then, and when I first saw him, I immediately recognized him as the spiritual master I had long been seeking, without any real hope of finding such a person. The recognition had come as a shock, unexpected and startling. From that moment my life changed.

My first visit to Pune was for a little over three weeks. When Osho initiated me into sannyas, he suggested that I participate in psychotherapy groups. At that time, the only therapy group available was the AUM Marathon encounter group.

I had entered the group knowing nothing of psychotherapy, let alone the encounter groups that were becoming widely known in London and America. But with the AUM Marathon, and during the daily program of meditation at the ashram, I experienced wonders that I had only previously read about. I had never considered that the marvels of inner reality could be experienced by somebody as ordinary as me. In just a few short days, my inner world opened its doors. The group, the meditation, the wonder of Osho's presence – everything on my first visit confirmed that I wanted to live close to Osho in his ashram in Pune.

I returned to England where it took two years to arrange this momentous shift in my life. I came back to Pune, to live and work in Osho's ashram, in December 1978. At the time of eating my banana, I had been the ashram dentist for a year.

As I breakfasted happily, I became aware that somebody else had come to sit beside me. Turning, I was surprised to see Vivek, Osho's personal caretaker, on my right side.

In those days, she rarely left Lao Tzu House except

The First Time

to accompany Osho to his morning discourse in Buddha Hall, and to darshans, those personal meetings, up close and direct with the master, where Osho would meet with new arrivals, people departing, and group participants. Vivek was a silent, shadowy figure, usually a few steps behind him, ever gently vigilant. I had never had occasion to be close to her.

"Hi Devageet." Her voice was light, and ... English. It was unexpected; I hadn't known she was English. She was beautiful.

"What do you think about electric tooth brushing?" she asked suddenly.

I swallowed a huge mouthful of banana sandwich while summoning my thoughts on the subject. I had been a dentist for sixteen years and such conversations were commonplace for me, so it was easy to rattle on happily about the virtues and vices of various types of brushing methods, and other aspects of oral hygiene, while enjoying the close proximity of two attractive women. Somewhere far in the background, I could feel Sagaro's emotions were definitely protective. I guessed that she sensed a threat to our relationship.

I finished speaking and Vivek looked directly into my eyes, before saying, "Do you think you could examine Osho's teeth?"

My stomach lurched, and my breathing nearly stopped. Was it fear, or excitement? My voice moved up a couple of octaves as I answered. "Well, yes, sure I can look at Osho's teeth; after all, teeth are teeth. But whenever I have been close to him in darshan my body does strange things. My legs tremble, and once I became cross-eyed. At one of Osho's birthday darshans, my legs became so rubbery I couldn't stand or walk for twenty minutes. I had to be carried away."

At that celebration, many who had come to sit in front of Osho also needed to be carried away. A queue of thousands waited for his blessing, many unable to move away after touching Osho's feet. A team of 'lifters' kept the long line moving.

Vivek laughed merrily. I could not help noticing the orthodontic arrangement of her upper incisors. Being a dentist had created a unique observation platform from where I viewed the world. "He's just an ordinary man. You can ask his doctor, Amrito[1]. He will tell you that you just have to treat Osho like anybody else. He is just an ordinary man."

I was to hear that phrase many times, in many widely differing situations, over the next twelve years.

I shrugged, trying to allow my delight at her invitation to overcome my fears of inadequacy. "Mmm," I said doubtfully. "I can hear what you are saying, and that may be true for you. Maybe that's because you're used to it, but when I got close my body did weird things. Trying to be a dentist with crossed-eyes and jelly legs may prove difficult." I joked, but the physical effects were

---

1. Devaraj's name was later changed to Amrito by Osho

true. "I'm a bit nervous – even the thought of looking in his mouth makes me shaky – but I would love to give it a go."

I could see by her smile that she dismissed my comments. Perhaps being in Osho's presence had become commonplace for her. I had only been really close to him while sitting at his feet during the evening darshans.

"Have you lived in Australia?" she asked. My words had triggered another train of thought in her.

I smiled self consciously, "Yep. Good onya. Only for a couple of years but it left a deep impression, especially on my vocabulary."

She nodded and again smiled, before saying, "Okay."

Then, refocusing her mind, she briskly instructed me to be ready and waiting at the gates of the Lao-Tzu House at 5:00 p.m., freshly showered and robed, with whatever dental instruments I would need. "Do you need anything special in his room?" she enquired. Until that moment I had not grasped that the examination would not take place in the ashram dental office. His room! My mind wobbled on its axis.

"I will need a good light," I managed to say.

"He has lights in his room, you know, for reading. Will they be okay?" she asked.

"Well, yes, I suppose so, provided I can move one close enough to his mouth so I can see inside." I replied.

I could see that she had not pictured the actuality of a dental examination. Who does? Again, she dismissed any doubts saying, "I'll get Haridas to fix something up." I knew Haridas, a tall handsome German, who was Osho's handyman and electrician.

"And," she lowered her voice conspiratorially, "it's important to keep the meeting secret. Nobody is to know, not even your girlfriend." She moved her head a little to indicate Sagaro sitting on my other side. "We protect Osho's privacy very carefully. It's an important part of keeping him safe, you know, his security." Her large eyes grew larger as she spoke, great grey-blue orbs gazing into mine. Then, she rose quickly, and left.

I was left trying to grasp what she had just said. What had privacy and security to do with dentistry? I turned to look at my girlfriend. Sagaro was pale. I wondered what she had heard. Clearly, I could not tell her what had just taken place. Vivek's last words had dropped between Sagaro and me like a screen.

"I must rush to work now, I'm late. Bye love. See you for lunch." The words came tumbling out as I gave her a quick hug before sprinting to the ashram dental office.

I was ten minutes late, and already there was a queue of people, nursing a variety of dental emergencies, sitting on a narrow wooden bench in the small alley outside of the dental office. The alley fore-court served as our dental waiting room. Sitting at an open window facing them was my dental receptionist, Anado.

Anado was tall, taller than me, willowy, a

glamorous, smouldering-eyed Italian beauty. I had heard gossip that she had been a promising film starlet. The same source told me she was the great-great-great-great grand niece of Machiavelli. All of which was fascinating, but not the usual qualification for a dental receptionist. Anado's dental experience was nil. But the Rajneesh Ashram dental office was an unusual dental frontier outpost.

At its opening, I had asked Vidya, the ashram work coordinator, for a dental receptionist "with experience, or at least a bit of dental knowledge." Vidya was South African, and with the humour peculiar to that country, had selected Anado, who knew even less about dentistry than herself.

Anado was not only taller than me, but louder too. Her four-year-old, powerfully compact son was louder than both of us together. Daily, in the echoing confines of the small alley that served as the dental waiting room, he would scream, rage, bellow and howl for chocolate, while the waiting patients cringed as his volume added to their misery.

His head did not quite reach to the sill of the window where his mother sat, unapproachable, fronted by her large blue dental appointment book. Undaunted, he regularly and powerfully gave full, molto–vibrato voice to his frustration while simultaneously clawing madly for the hand-hold that would enable him to glimpse the woman who was withholding the sweetness he craved.

The First Time

His remarkably venal vocabulary, sheer persistence, and unbelievably powerful vocal outrage directed towards an unheeding existence, created a daily elemental traumatic experience that my patients remembered long after their dental crisis had passed.

Seeing me arrive late, Anado asked in a challenging tone, "Eh, Devageet! Why are you late?"

I had been hoping to avoid that question. "I can't tell you," I replied, galloping past her window to take my place in the tiny dental office. My operating stool was directly behind her receptionist's chair.

She raised her magnificent eyebrows, and lifted her aquiline nostrils to the sky, before speaking to the assembled, captive, dental multitude. "'E cannot tell us why 'e kept us all a-waiting! Who the fuck does 'e think 'e is? God?" Nobody spoke. She filled the rhetorical vacuum with a gust of fluent Italian invective that followed my entry into the shaded, but already hot, dental room.

My two chair side assistants, Ahuti and Ashu, were ostentatiously busying themselves, unnecessarily clattering the steel instruments in their sterilizing trays, clearly bursting with unspoken curiosity. I had never been late before, and as they had passed on their way to work they could not have missed seeing me sitting on the Zen wall speaking to Vivek. This was high quality gossip, and the ashram loved gossip. It was the currency valued beyond all else, except perhaps enlightenment.

Interrupting Anado's dramatic flow I casually

announced to her, "Oh yes, and I need you to cancel my last two patients. I have to leave at four." Then, swiftly cutting off any further questions, I asked for the first emergency patient to be sent in.

The day passed with unspoken questions squirming and seething into every gap and pause in our busy dental schedule. At four o'clock, after surreptitiously trying to gather my examination instruments, along with a towel, a bib, and a dental chart, I nonchalantly hurried from the dental office before Anado could harangue me with more unanswerable questions.

In those days, I lived at the Dutch Palace, a name that carried echoes of a long-forgotten magnificence. The large building had descended into semi-ruin with little more than its size and crumbling facade to hint that behind its threadbare, posthumous grandeur, were faded glories rooted in the British Raj.

The larger of the two huge downstairs ballrooms carried a ghostly, almost ghastly, hint of what used to be. On the first floor, where I lived, the glory had long since gone, leaving only fat cockroaches living in the cracked plaster, and defunct plumbing.

Despite the building's seriously distressed gentility, I enjoyed my room with its terracotta tiled, roofed balcony that overlooked the large, dusty garden that separated the main house from the busy street and the railway next door. Seated on my veranda, reclining in my dusty, musty, rattan armchair, listening to the honking rickshaws and street sellers, I could look up at the shredded awning and monsoon screens made from ancient matting. I was a regular observer of the frequent gladiatorial encounters between the resident giant praying mantis, and the gecko family that was seeking to challenge its territorial imperative.

On this special day, I ran up the wrought iron spiral staircase that hung precariously to the outside brick wall. On my way, I passed the scorched and blackened tangle of wires that served as the first floor's electrical junction box. I fervently hoped that there would be water in my large bathroom.

Despite its many taps, spouts, drains, cracked basins, zinc buckets, ineffectual rotted, rubber plungers, floor-scrubbing brushes, odd bits of stinking, kinked wire used frequently to unblock drains that resisted our efforts, there was rarely any water. By then I had become wise enough to keep a bucket under the endlessly dripping taps, thus saving enough water for such emergencies. But I was lucky: I was in time for the four o'clock dribble.

I showered carefully, making sure my soap was non-perfumed, because Osho was allergic to perfume. As an added precaution, I wiped my skin with half a lime. Quickly drying myself, I put on my best orange robe, and gathering my thoughts and dental instruments, quickly made my way to the noisy street to hail a passing rickshaw.

Every aspect of living in Pune and working in the ashram was exotic and fun. I would regularly catch myself thinking, "If only my mother could see me now!"

Arriving back at the ashram I made my way to Lao Tzu Gate, where Osho lived. The gate guard looked up in mild curiosity, clearly waiting for me to explain myself. I stayed silent.

"You want something, Devageet?" he asked pointedly.

"Err, I'm meeting Vivek," I said, wondering if this breached our secrecy arrangement.

"Has she made an appointment with you?" he asked, knowing the absurdity of the question: what could Vivek possibly have to say to me?

"In a way," I answered.

He was growing irritated with my hesitancy. "Well, did she or didn't she?"

"Yes, she did," I said, wishing she would come and save me from this ordeal.

At this point Vivek walked out of a small side door a few yards behind the guard. Hearing her steps as she approached the gate, he hurried to unbolt it, allowing me access. I entered the sacred precincts, and Vivek led me to the shoe rack beside the door from which she had emerged. I heard the gate creak behind us as it clanged shut.

I took off my Birkenstocks and put on the socks Vivek had instructed me to bring for use in the house corridors. My heart was pounding. My mind was strangely blank. She led me inside, waiting briefly as I hopped from one foot to the other while struggling to put on my socks. I was almost finished when she walked into the house, clearly expecting me to follow.

My first impression of Lao Tzu House was its immense silence. Then I took in its shining cleanliness. As I walked, I saw thousands of books neatly standing in bookcases that lined the walls from floor to ceiling.

I followed as Vivek led me along a red-tiled corridor, passing several doors along the way. Through one open doorway, I noticed gleaming stainless steel pots and pans, and marble counters. I guessed it was Osho's kitchen.

Passing another door, almost opposite the kitchen, I saw the household entrance to Chuang Tzu Auditorium, where Osho gave nightly darshan, and occasionally public morning discourses, when he wasn't using the newly-built, but as yet unfinished, Buddha Hall Auditorium.

I was backstage in Osho's house and about to meet my Master face to face. I was trembling, more with excitement than nervousness.

The corridor opened into an atrium, with a curved marble staircase on my left, leading upwards to the first floor. In front of me were two big wooden, outer doors, and on my right, two floor-to-ceiling plate glass doors. Vivek stopped before the glass doors. She instructed me to remove my socks, then pushed open the doors and ushered me through.

Inside, as I looked to my left, I noticed Osho's simple, elegant black, hand-made sandals placed carefully outside a shining, plain wooden door. What little thinking I was still capable of promptly deserted me at the sight of his sandals. I heard Vivek tell me that I should remain standing where I was until I was called. I nodded dumbly.

She opened the wooden door and disappeared inside. Within a few seconds her head reappeared and she motioned me to enter Osho's room.

The room was like none I had ever seen before. The first glance showed me floor and walls made of warm, pinkish marble, tiger-striped with deep, thick veins of grey. The only furniture was a very large, immaculate bed with two beautifully designed bedside lamps.

On the left was a complete wall of rosewood-fronted, fitted wardrobes. Vivek was standing on my right in a large, square, bay-windowed part of the room. Osho was next to her, sitting in a high-backed armchair.

He was smiling, his eyes twinkling. I namasted, and he returned my greeting. *"Hello Geet,"* he said softly.

My first and only thought was, "That's not my name. My name is Devageet."

As if reading my tottering mind, he then said, *"You have come to examine my teeth, Devageet?"* More a statement than a question.

My many first impressions were superimposed on each other. I noticed that his head was shinier than I had ever seen it, as if there was light shining directly on it, although the venetian blinds covering the windows were closed.

His voice was so soft, and I realized that I had previously only heard it amplified through a microphone and loudspeakers. The quality of his voice, its tone and timbre, was wonderfully soothing and gentle. I wondered if, noticing my brain-free state, he was using his voice to put me at ease. In fact, I felt very at ease and immensely, intensely happy. It was only that my mind had ceased most of its usual functions.

I managed to nod.

I noticed that Osho was seated next to a revolving wooden bookcase of a Victorian design exactly like one I had owned in England. I was strangely delighted – I had loved that bookcase.

The bookcase was full of books. On top of it, next to a round, lacquered wooden pot full of exquisite fountain pens, were three beautiful wristwatches, and a pile of a dozen or more books that appeared to be in current use.

Opposite where he was sitting was a state-of-the-art Bang and Olufsen music centre in a cabinet of deep, shining rosewood. I had owned one of those too.

He appeared smaller than I expected. In discourse and darshan, I had always seen Osho as tall. Instead, his actual physical size was very similar to my own. I guessed it was his energetic presence and charisma that gave the impression of sheer physical size.

These general impressions took only a moment to become etched on my passive mind.

"Do you have everything you need, Devageet?" his

voice softly enquired.

Again I nodded, before adding, "Except that I will need a light to see into your mouth."

Osho looked at Vivek. She moved to a table lamp some ten feet from where he sat. Holding it up, she asked, "Will this do?"

I nodded, before adding, "It will do provided it will reach closer to Osho's mouth. I need to be able to see his teeth inside."

She tugged at the lead, grimacing, muttering, "I forgot to ask Haridas. It's too short to reach. Maybe I can get an extension lead."

In my state of minimal brain function, I simply stood there, happily inert. Vivek was holding the dentally-useless lamp. Osho simply watched, then asked, *"Could you use a flashlight, Devageet?"*

"Yes, provided it will shine to the back of your mouth," I said.

"Vivek, bring the penlight, the one I use for darshan," he instructed.

Vivek brought the small silver penlight that I had often seen Osho using as an energy-moving device on some people during darshan. He would shine it on their third eye centre, or occasionally on their throat centre.

Vivek lifted his thickly luxuriant moustache and held the penlight between his lips, close to his lower teeth. He opened his mouth just wide enough for me to peer inside. Yes, I could see enough to make a reasonably accurate dental examination.

I nodded, saying, "It's great, but you'll have to hold the light steady, Vivek. I will go behind Osho, and look into his mouth from there."

I moved to the back, behind his chair, and opened the rolled towel containing my dental mirror, tweezers, and probe. Leaning over his right shoulder, with his head almost beneath my left arm, in a classic old-style dental posture, I tapped and prodded my way around Osho's teeth.

He sat unusually still, nothing moved at all. His eyelids were closed and the large eyes beneath were utterly immobile. His tongue was motionless throughout. He never even swallowed. Everything in his mouth was pink and healthy, young, responsive and alive, but astonishingly unmoving. It was remarkable.

As I worked I became aware that the silence in the room had deepened.

After completing my examination I said, "I've looked at your teeth, Osho."

He opened his large, shining eyes slowly, and asked, *"Can you fix them?"*

"Yes, there's not much that needs doing," I replied. He asked, *"When?"*

Somewhat confused at the speed things were moving, I answered, "Now, if you like."

Vivek, following this rapid exchange, broke in saying, "Okay Devageet. We will have to make special arrangements before fixing an actual time and date."

Osho smiled, inclining his head a little, and then said, *"You let Vivek take care. She will arrange everything."*

I gathered my dental instruments together in the towel, folding the dental chart carefully. Vivek took the penlight from his mouth.

She turned to me and, taking my hand gently but firmly, led me towards the door, saying, "You wait next door in my room, and I will come in a few minutes and we can discuss the next steps."

I turned and namasted Osho as I reached the door to his room. He was smiling. I could feel myself smiling too, a smile almost too big for my lips to contain.

Vivek took me along the short corridor that connected her room to Osho's. Her room was larger than his, and her bed was covered in a sumptuous silk cover. She told me to sit and wait for her.

I sat amidst the luxurious surroundings in a strange state of full awareness, but without any of my normal thought processes. The impressions were filling the screen of my mind unimpeded by judgments or comparisons. It was a state of open awareness accompanied by euphoric stillness and peace.

Directly in front of me was a bathroom, similar in size to the one in the room I rented in the Dutch Palace. The difference was that this one was pristine clean, and I guessed that the many taps had the advantage of supplying water.

The First Time

I became aware of the head of a mop moving rhythmically in and out of my field of vision from behind the bathroom door. A vivacious-looking young woman, with short, dark blond hair and very large teeth that grinned at me, quickly followed the mop. I guessed that this was Vivek's cleaner.

Moments later, Vivek reappeared. She carefully closed the bathroom door before speaking. "Devageet, you will not immediately understand, but we take special care of Osho. Nothing for him is as simple as for other people. We take great care of his privacy, his health, and his safety."

She looked into my eyes as she spoke, presumably to see if I was taking in what she was saying. I nodded, for her to see that somebody was alive and responsive behind my happy eyes.

Thus reassured, she continued, "We will need to get new instruments. He cannot use instruments that others have used."

I murmured that in the ashram dental office we took great care to sterilize our instruments after every use. I was proud of the sterilizing system we had set up; it was no mean feat in India.

She quickly added that it wasn't a question of sterility, but of newness, adding that she took care that nothing Osho used had been previously owned by anybody else. He didn't even like to read secondhand books.

This was a whole new world for me.

The First Time

"We will have to arrange a suitable time for his dental session, a time when nobody else would be around … maybe we can do it during morning discourse?" She was thinking aloud, while I listened. Somewhere in my depths I was amazed even at the concept of cancelling Osho's morning discourse.

"Yes, we can have all the sannyasins in Buddha Hall,[1] and then close the ashram main gate, and the guards can make sure that nobody accidentally intrudes while you are working on Osho." She stopped speaking, and then said, "You can begin to get an idea that taking care of Osho is not as simple as people believe. We have to ensure his security and safety in everything he does. But, although you need to know it, this does not really concern you. You just wait for me or Laxmi (Osho's secretary) to contact you about the next step. We will take care of everything. But," and she leaned forward, so close I could feel her breath, before saying emphatically, "nobody, but nobody, must know about his dental treatment; not your girlfriend, not anybody. Do you understand?"

I nodded, before adding, "I will have to let Ashu know. She's my dental nurse. She will be helping me when I work on Osho's teeth."

Vivek said, "I will take care of that too. I will tell Ashu when the time is right. Meanwhile you be very careful that nobody knows about today."

---

1. Meditation hall used for Osho talks and meditation sessions.

I again nodded happily.

Vivek then led me back along the red corridor and out onto the pathway. As I put on my sandals before she left, she said, with a twinkle, "Remember, our little secret!"

Her words were still echoing around my brain as the Lao Tzu Gate guard slid the iron bolt to let me out. I was back in the ashram world.

Vasumati, one of the ashram therapists was passing. She looked at me, gasped, flushed red, and then screamed, "Devageet! You've just seen Osho!"

I was shocked. My befuddled brain took valuable microseconds to overcome the blast of disbelief and alarm at her words. "Ssshh!" I whispered in horror. "Be quiet! It's a secret. Nobody must know. And … how did you know?" I said in her ear.

"It's obvious. It's written all over your face!"

Only later did I realize that sharing a secret with Vasumati had the same effect as putting it on national television.

Chapter 2
Sheela's Misplaced Effort

One afternoon in 1980, soon after I had started working as Osho's personal dentist, Sheela summoned me to a meeting in Laxmi's office in the Pune ashram. Sheela was acting as stand-in for Laxmi, Osho's full-time Indian secretary, who was in Delhi negotiating for the purchase of land for the new commune in India. The number of Osho's sannyasins was increasing very fast and rapidly outgrowing the property in Pune. Osho had instructed Laxmi to find a larger property, big enough for him to create a new style of commune – not an ashram in any traditional sense – where his vision for a totally new human consciousness, based on meditation, would become reality.

At the meeting, Sheela was attended by her support team – Asha, Vidya, Isabel, Padma and Homa, and others. She solemnly announced that none of them could work with me any longer.

I was taken completely by surprise at her words. I had never worked with any of them.

Despite being ambushed and outnumbered, I resorted to male reasoning. I pointed out that what she said couldn't possibly be true because I didn't actually work with any of them and never had. This point, despite its obvious relevance, only served to irritate Sheela further, and demonstrate to her my clearly objectionable qualities.

In condemning tones, backed up with stony stares, she told me she was going to inform Osho of her conclusions that very evening when she saw him to review the day's work in the ashram. Darkly and dismissive, Sheela added that she would give me his answer by tomorrow. Her look indicated, game, set, and match!

I felt well and truly stitched up. I had no understanding of what was behind Sheela's dislike of me, nor why she chose to magnify her personal dislike by including other people in it, people I barely knew, and had little contact with. Nor did I know why she wanted to bring this piece of bad-tempered judgment to Osho. I guessed she was demonstrating her power – to me, and to the other women present. Sheela liked to demonstrate her power.

She had given me no opportunity to defend myself against her "outrageous slings and arrows," merely presented them to my face. I could only trust that Osho would see through her strategies.

Sheela called me early the next day. There were fewer people in her office this time. Without preamble, and barely a glance in my direction, she began: "Osho has told me to give you this message:

> '*I want all my people to work together, in harmony, without jealousy. Devageet will never get rid of Sheela. Sheela will never get rid of Devageet. They are both important in my work.*

In my new commune, Devageet will be the head of the new dental hospital. It is important for my commune that you work together. And remember, I love you all, whatever part you play.'"

She put the paper down and swiveled her chair away from me. I guessed that I had been dismissed.

I left her office feeling deeply relieved, overjoyed to feel loved and understood by Osho, and smiling happily at his adroit brilliance. My trust that he would see the truth, despite Sheela's efforts to manipulate him, had proven greater than my fear of her powers of administrative authority.

As I walked away back to the ashram dental office, I marveled at his deft touch. Sheela herself had to give me the message detailing Osho's support for me. She had no other option because the message supporting me contained his message of support for her. And the last part of his message, *"And remember, I love you all, whatever part you play in the work,"* was a reminder that, whatever my role in Osho's commune, dentist or not, I was loved. And, so was Sheela.

From the moment I had become Osho's dentist, being close to him, as well as deepening Sheela's hatred of me, had caused my own feelings of unworthiness to surface. I never felt worthy of being his dentist. To me he was always so beautiful, intelligent, compassionate, graceful and unfailingly loving. In the mirror of his presence, I often felt myself to be graceless, lumpen, and emotionally gross. I put it down to his compassion that he allowed me near him. Osho was the first person I had known who loved me as I was, unconditionally, but it was years before I could give that degree of loving to myself.

Chapter 3
Love and Dentistry

In September 1981, I was living on Rancho Rajneesh, Osho's new commune in Oregon, United States. (formerly known as the Big Muddy Ranch). After not having seen Osho for over four months since his departure from Pune, I was not even certain that I was still his dentist.

I had arrived at the Big Muddy in the middle of August 1981. Osho was still living in New Jersey. I was invited to help prepare the huge ranch in case Osho chose to make it his temporary home. During my few weeks at the ranch, I had already been a builder, farmer, gardener and traffic controller.

Osho arrived at the Big Muddy at the beginning of September. He promptly renamed it Rancho Rajneesh. The closest I had been to him was standing at the side of the dirt road with my hands folded in namaste at the dust cloud stirred up by his Rolls Royce as he zoomed past on his twice-daily drives.

One evening, a few weeks after Osho's arrival, Dolma, the ashram work coordinator, asked as I was returning from my day's work with the trailer erection crew, why I was not fixing up Osho's new dental room. Surprised, I told her that I didn't even know there was a dental room. Nobody had thought to tell me.

I asked where it was located. There were no residential buildings yet. The seventy people working on the ranch lived in a conglomeration of tents we had named "Tent City," and the trailer crew was busily leveling sites for the first residential trailers for workers to arrive. By way of an answer, Dolma told me to see Vivek in Osho's triplewide trailer situated in the newly-named, Lao-Tsu valley, a beautiful valley about three miles further along the John Day River.

As I made my way there, I was thinking that Sheela's antagonism to me would surely prevent any priority being given to the construction of a dental room. In Pune, she had deliberately tried to hinder my work by telling Osho that she found me impossible to work with and that I had purchased unnecessarily expensive dental materials. Without knowing her agenda, I guessed she would try to hinder my work with Osho in any way she could. Her attitude towards me was no worse than how she treated any person who had direct close contact with him: the closer the contact the greater her belligerence. She seemed to reserve special vituperation for men. I took her attitude as an "abrasion" device of the type used by Gurdjieff in his commune. In this way, each confrontation helped me to see those parts of my ego that only Sheela and her cronies could stir up.

Later, over a cup of tea, Vivek told me that Osho had himself designed his personal trailer to include a tiny dental room directly behind his living quarters. I was somewhat stunned at both his creativity and his focus on our dental sessions, and amused at how he brilliantly managed to sidestep any anti-dental plans Sheela may have been considering.

Vivek also made it clear that whatever other work I was doing on the ranch, my real job was to get Osho's dental room together. "After all you're his dentist."

I set to work, ordering equipment and organizing the carpentry and the special reinforcement of the trailer floor needed to support the heavy dental chair and x-ray equipment. During the weeks of designing and equipping Osho's dental room, I was also creating a separate dental suite for commune residents in a medical trailer known as Pythagoras.

My slumbering sense of dental inferiority was startled into awakening upon the arrival at Rancho Rajneesh of Nirvan, a fully-fledged dental professor. He was a crown-and-bridge expert and all-round dental Renaissance man and creative whiz: He designed his own spectacles, grew his own cattle for beef, designed and largely built his own house, and had even founded his own religion, with himself as chief priest.

Nirvan and I had first met in Pune a couple of years before, shortly after my own arrival as a resident of the ashram. He had set up the original ashram dental room on his retirement from United States dentistry, with surgery equipment imported from the United States. He had been setting up the dental office for several months before I had arrived.

I had intended to live at the ashram in Pune as a simple disciple, a plain and ordinary man. Dentistry for me was over, it was a part of my former, pre-Osho life. My idea was to be a disciple, to work as a gardener, carrying water and chopping wood, as in the Zen stories I had read.

I had been a general dental practitioner in England and Australia for the past seventeen years. Working in the English health service was arduous, uncreative, boring, and overloaded with paperwork. In Australia, I had lightened my burden by painting and reading philosophy between dental appointments, but working like this was limiting, and I desperately wanted to live in a way that would enable me to have personal experience of my inner sacred self. On meeting Osho it had happened, and continues to happen.

My dream was to live as close to Osho as I could manage.

In Pune, after a few days of getting settled into a small apartment in "the Dutch Palace," I was ready for my new life in the ashram. I applied for work to Vidya, the ashram work coordinator. "Be a dentist," she told me. I protested, saying that I was finished with dentistry, muttering that I wanted to be a simple disciple in the presence of my master. She gave me a withering look, made more powerfully bleak by her pale blue eyes piercingly observing me from their perch above her powerful nose. She repeated herself briefly and sharply, "Devageet, be a dentist."

I continued mumbling that Nirvan's dental office was barely big enough for one dentist, never mind two. And that Nirvan was more than able to … Vidya interrupted, leaning forward and looking into my eyes even more penetratingly with her steely orbs, before repeating slowly, with great effect: "Devageet – be – a – dentist. And tell Nirvan that you will be his assistant."

I had walked to the small room that served as the soon-to-be dental office for sannyasins. Showing me the dental machines he had carefully set up, Nirvan had initially been friendly and mellow, happy to show a fellow professional his fine cabinetry and gadgetry. I was very impressed by his woodworking skills and general expertise. The first day we worked together in Pune, he had casually complained about "those bitches in the front office." The next day he complained bitterly about his loss of erectile function "due to this fucking heat," and how he couldn't stop farting: "God, man, my wind is like rotten eggs. Those fucking amoebas and giardia in my guts are sucking out all my life juices." He painted a vivid picture of his virile decline due to an invasion by tropical intestinal parasites.

On my third day as his assistant, Nirvan announced that he was leaving Pune for America. He generously offered to sell me his vast stock of vitamins, unbelievable quantities of dental floss, exotic Californian food supplements, and a fine, but over-priced, foam-and-coconut fibre mattress of his own design. I had to decline his offer due to my poverty but I was impressed by the quality and quantity of his possessions.

With Nirvan's departure to the United States I had become the Pune ashram dentist. One year later, in January 1979, I had become Osho's personal dentist. After Nirvan's departure, I mused that he occasionally may have regretted leaving Pune, perhaps imagining that if he had stayed he would have been Osho's dentist instead of me.

When Nirvan arrived at Rancho Rajneesh in 1981, Dolma had unknowingly reversed our original ashram roles by assigning him as my assistant. She instructed him to help me design and build clinical dental rooms for sannyasins in Pythagoras, the communal medical trailer.

It took only a few days for Nirvan to attempt a dental coup. He sabotaged our mutually agreed upon plans, stating to me emphatically that whatever dental knowledge I had was of no value. I tried to compromise but his attitude was unbending. I had little alternative but to refer the matter to Dolma, in her role as ranch work coordinator. She decided on the spot that the three of us – Dolma, Nirvan, and myself – needed an urgent meeting to "sort things out."

The meeting took place in the dusty main street of Rancho Rajneesh. Nirvan robustly restated that I was a mere dental pygmy compared to his superior qualifications and experience. He made a forceful pitch that on Rancho

Rajneesh, he should be the person in charge of all things dental. "Christ, Dolma, the guy isn't even American. He is unqualified!" He went on, powerfully making the point that his clear academic superiority made it obvious that I was not, and could never hope to become, his equal.

As I contemplated his argument, I realized that his observations, despite being made with much spray and emphasis, were undeniably true. However, Dolma rejected them, saying, "Nirvan, this is a mystery school, not a dental campus." At that, he had shaken his head before stumping off into the dust, each step showing his disgruntled resentment.

Deliberating on the situation later, I realized that in America, Osho could, and should, have the very finest of dental treatment. I decided to write him a letter offering to stand aside, and asked Vivek to deliver it.

In my letter, I explained that by United States standards, my dental skills were modest. I told him I understood that in Pune I may have been the best dentist available due to the poor general standards of dentistry there, but now, in America, where practically every family had a crown-and-bridge specialist as a son-in-law, he could have the best and most highly qualified personal dentist, with much higher qualifications than I possessed.

Vivek, always plain spoken and often brutally direct, had raised her fine eyebrows and looked at me as though I was mentally challenged as I explained the nature of the message I was asking her to deliver. In those days, since his arrival in America, Osho had declared himself to be in a period of public silence; messages for him were delivered as letters, usually by Sheela. But in this case, as we stood in the tiny dental office behind his living room, Vivek personally delivered my note.

Within moments she was back. "Devageet, here's Osho's reply to your letter:

> *'Devageet, don't be such a fool. You are not my dentist because you are the best dentist in the world. You are my personal dentist because your love for me makes your work perfect. P.S. The other dentist has bad breath.'"*

I cried and laughed together.

Chapter 4
Only Skidding

It was early October 1981. Oregon, USA. Osho was driving his white Rolls Royce twice each day, once in the morning and once later, in the afternoon. He always drove to the same place: the Madras weighing station.

Madras was a small hick town some forty miles from Rancho Rajneesh. I had arrived there in August, the day the local newspaper, the Madras Pioneer, carried the headline: "Another Jonestown." Clearly somebody on the editorial board had an agenda for Osho's people. Sheela had been authorised by Osho to purchase a suitable property for his people in the United States She had purchased the Big Muddy Ranch only a few weeks earlier, and the headlines already suggested how the local media wanted to corral local opinion.

The weighing station was outside the town on the road to Antelope. Osho would drive the nineteen miles from the ranch to Antelope, and then take the pretty Willowdale Road before heading out on the highway to Madras. The roads were mainly empty, with scenery that was pure American Gothic.

I was working as a traffic coordinator, alongside Tapodana and Venu. We coordinated the movements of the outgoing and incoming vehicles on Rancho Rajneesh.

Since the entry road was too narrow for two vehicles to pass, or even for large trucks, it took delicate manoeuvring to prevent any foul-ups.

As well as being traffic coordinators we had numerous other functions, including acting as the ranch communications centre, taking all incoming telephone calls. We also monitored all handheld Motorola transmissions, staying in touch with the various sannyasin work teams on their widely dispersed and often remote ranch locations. One hundred and twenty-six square miles is a big area, and frequently work teams needed help in contacting other working units. Each of us also took turns in going off the ranch to do the various delivery and collecting jobs that came up.

On the day in question I was going to Madras to take delivery of a medical item.

I was cruising happily in an old blue Volvo sedan. The sun was shining, although the day was cold and clear. It was fall. Driving to Antelope, the road was dusty, scattered with rocks that had tumbled down from the hills bordering the narrow, twisty trail that had been upgraded into a road. Mostly, the way was not wide enough for two cars, especially on the bends.

The previous day, I had been on a similar errand. In the distance I had seen a fast moving dust cloud: a vehicle was approaching very rapidly. Looking at my watch, I guessed it might be Osho returning from his afternoon drive. I had immediately pulled off the road,

Only Skidding

sheltering beneath an overhanging bluff. Moments later, the big white Rolls Royce roared past in a cloud of dust.

Yes, it was Osho. I had to smile. In my imagination he drove like a mystic on his way to the great beyond, and nothing was going to stand in his way. Whoosh!

Later that day, Vivek called me from Lao Tzu House, where she and Osho now lived. She asked me to meet her there. It was unusual, but I guessed she wanted to speak about the new dental room that I was setting up for Osho. I was wrong.

"Devageet," she began, looking pale and serious. It was hard for me to take it seriously though because she looked so beautiful. "You were driving too fast!"

My jaw must have hung open in disbelief.

She went on: "You know you shouldn't be on the road when Osho is driving."

I vaguely remembered that we had been given a directive to keep the roads clear during his drive, at least as much as possible. She waited for my reply.

"Well ... it's true, I forgot that you were out, on the road. But as soon as I saw the Rolls coming I pulled over.," I admitted, adding, "I was actually stopped when you passed."

She barely registered my words. "You were driving too fast! You narrowly missed causing an accident." She surveyed my face, perhaps looking for guilt, but I felt good with myself, knowing that there had been no risk.

"You need to be more aware when you drive." That

was certainly true, and not just about driving. "In future, just make sure that you drive more slowly and keep off the Antelope Road when Osho is out for his drive."

I smiled, but she didn't smile back. She turned away. Our meeting was clearly over. Vivek was definitely grumpy. Beautiful, but grumpy.

It was the next day. I was driving out past Antelope, enjoying the sunlight shining on the golden aspens, and feeling so full of joy it was almost painful. Tears brimmed my eyes, yet laughter was bubbling unreasonably in my belly. I was singing to myself. In an empty car I loved to sing at the top of my voice.

I had just turned onto the Willowdale Road when I noticed a pick-up approaching fast in the other lane. As it came closer, I saw four figures in the cab, three men with a woman between them. Hung on the back wall of the cab were two hunting rifles. As the vehicle passed me I noticed that the woman was strikingly like Vivek.

Still singing lustily, I looked in my rear-view mirror and saw that the pick-up had screeched in a tight u-turn and was coming up fast behind me. I stopped singing.

The vehicle pulled alongside and the driver signalled me to pull over. As I did so, he braked next to me. All three men got out, one was carrying a rifle, and the woman … was Vivek.

She ran towards me, saying, "Devageet! Quick! Osho has had an accident. Quick! We must get back to him right away!"

She pulled open the door of the old blue Volvo and jumped in. I leaped in beside her and we roared off into the sunlit haze. In my mirror I noticed the men getting back into their truck.

Vivek was very anxious. "For God's sake, go faster! Can't this bloody old crate go any faster? Put your bloody foot down!"

I managed a wry smile; only yesterday this gorgeous grumpy woman was telling me that I drove too fast, today I was driving too slow. "Okay Vivek. But this Volvo is a poor old beast, and I've got my foot through the floorboards. How far away is it? And what happened? Is he hurt?"

"It's a few miles along this road. We skidded on a patch of black ice. I told him he was going too fast, but he never listens." She spoke breathlessly, the words bumping into each other. "He drives like the wind. I get so afraid sometimes. He has no fear, none at all. I tell him to slow down but he either just smiles, or takes no notice. He skidded right off the road, almost into the river. The Rolls went right up onto a big rock. He's there now. The Rolls is completely stuck, and Osho is just sitting there. He's meditating! You've got to tell him to come into this car. I'll drive him to Antelope. You have to tell him to come back to Antelope with me." Her words were tumbling out fast and panicky.

I thought quickly. I had not met Osho face to face since he left Pune, months ago. The very idea that I could tell him, persuade him, to do something, seemed somehow absurd. I recognized this as yet another surreal Osho scenario, real, very real, and yet…

"Okay, I'll tell him. But if he's not hurt, and in no danger, why are you so worried?" I asked.

"He won't leave the car. He's so obstinate. He wants to wait for Avesh (Osho's driver and Rolls Royce technician) to come. He thinks I have gone to get Avesh, and that Avesh will fix the damage so that we can continue the drive. I hate having to leave Osho on his own. I get so frightened just leaving him in the middle of nowhere. Anything could happen."

Her loving concern shook me. Her words carried all the emotional overtones of a lover, a mother, a wife, a disciple, all wrapped together in one bundle of caring and responsibility. Osho was her whole life. He had had an accident and she was protecting him. Of course she was worried.

Twelve miles on she suddenly grabbed my arm and said pointing, "Look, there's the tree". Under the tree was a patch of black ice."

A large, mature willow tree hung drooping over the road. Within its shade was the sheen of black ice, and sure enough, I could see a long, straight, black skid mark. It led across the narrow highway, and there, perched on a rock, two feet clear off the ground, sheltered by golden aspens, was the big white Rolls Royce. Osho was sitting at the wheel.

Quickly I pulled across and parked the Volvo close by. Vivek half ran to the Rolls, turning to me, beseeching me to hurry as she did so. I could see Osho sitting in the driving seat motionless, relaxed, with his eyes closed. He was meditating.

This completed the sublime surrealism of the scene.

I approached his door. The window was closed. I knocked gently, not wanting to disturb his peace. He didn't move, and yet the window slid silently down. Opening his eyes, he turned and said with a smile, *"Hello Geet."*

In that moment, time stood still. He had said the same words to me on that day when I had entered his room in Pune for his first dental examination.

"Hello, Osho." I could only smile, intensely, bewilderingly happy.

Then I became aware of Vivek's anxiety flooding over me in waves.

"It looks as though you will need to come back to Antelope in the Volvo. Vivek will drive and I can stay here with the Rolls until Avesh comes.," I said, surprised at my own clarity.

He nodded, before saying, *"This door is stuck. It will not open."*

I tugged at it ineffectually, before saying, "I'll try to get the other door open."

The passenger door of the Rolls was jammed tight against three strands of barbed wire fencing that safeguarded a shallow river a few feet away. Vivek and I would have to pull down the barbed wire and flatten the undergrowth and stinging nettles in order to make a clear path for Osho to exit the levitated Rolls Royce. All four of its massive wheels were two feet off the ground. A very large rock was jammed tight into its transmission tunnel.

Vivek and I tugged the wire down, and took care to flatten the weeds and nettles. I carefully opened the door. Osho was already sliding across the seat, taking care that his full length knitted robe would not get caught around the automatic gearshift. Each of his movements was gentle and deliberate.

Vivek held out her hand to assist him. He took it as he stepped down. His light sandals were not suited to the damp undergrowth but he appeared not to notice as he made his way across the grass to the parked Volvo.

I stood, suddenly aware of being dressed in a cowboy hat, jeans, puffy down jacket, with calf-high boots. Seeing Osho, robed and graceful, holding Vivek's hand as they made their way to the car, was a sight I had seen before in very different circumstances, in his garden car porch in Pune as they returned from the morning discourse. Holding her hand as they made their way carried the flavour of unshakable serenity and love.

They were quickly gone. The old blue Volvo with its most unexpected passenger disappeared back along the empty road. I was left standing beside a massive white Rolls Royce, suspended two feet off the ground, in the middle of conservative, rural Oregon.

The driver of the first car that passed looked out, more casual than curious, then, as the bizarre sight registered, he took another long look, almost screwing his head from his shoulders, nearly giving himself a whiplash.

It was the same with other occasional cars that passed. Each driver looked, looked away, and then did a violent double take. But nobody stopped, until a small white van drew up. A number of Mexicans piled out, smiling and laughing, and intensely curious.

Walking around the Rolls, they spoke together in rapid Spanish. The smallest among them, the driver, came to me, saying in lilting tones, "Hey man, you in trouble?" His words, as he looked at the massive car suspended in the air beside us, even sounded funny to himself. He laughed out loud as I nodded, smiling.

"But it's okay. Help is on the way. They will lift it off," I said.

"Oh man, they will charge you a fortune. Oh man, we can help you get it back on the road. We can lift it off for you, no problem." He spoke in an attractive singsong.

This time I laughed out loud. "But this car weighs about eight tons," I said.

He laughed again. I noticed that although his body was small, his teeth were big and square, with an upper front incisor missing. While I noted his dental condition, he was saying, "No problem, we are strong, we can lift your car."

I shrugged, looking at his skinny body, and then stood back as they all took up positions around the Rolls. Taking the cue from their driver, they all heaved upwards simultaneously. The Rolls did not so much as budge.

Undaunted, the small man said to his team, "Okay, we need a lever. A big lever." And they scouted the thinly forested area until they found a young sapling.

"Hey man, this will do the trick." They cut it down with machetes that materialized from the back of their van. The denuded trunk was placed between the rock and the undercarriage of the levitated vehicle while the group of Mexicans applied their collective weight by sitting on the slim lever.

With a loud crack the trunk broke in two, and the team fell about grinning happily. "Okay man. You definitely need a pickup truck," said the driver with inexhaustible good humour. With those words, they all piled back into the small van and drove away.

Soon afterwards, two large, professional-looking tow trucks arrived. Avesh was sitting in the first one.

Under his direction, the tow team swiftly placed strong canvas loops beneath the Rolls before lifting it off the rock. While the car was in the air, Avesh winced as he looked closely at the mangled transmission. He radioed back to the ranch for Tapodana to send another rescue car to pick me up, and then from the cab of the leading tow truck, he gave a cheerful wave and drove off into the midday sun.

Standing there alone, I noticed the only signs of this strange event in rural Oregon, involving an enlightened mystic from India, a Rolls Royce, and three of his disciples, were a long skid mark, some flattened grass, a few strands of displaced barbed wire, and a rock enigmatically grooved by the flower of the British motor industry.

Chapter 5
Wading for the First Appointment

When the water came to Rancho Rajneesh from rains running off the many distant hills, it did not come as a friend. In this arid semi-desert, it came as a flash flood; a destructive torrent washing away flimsily held, sunbaked topsoil, undermining the precious riverbanks. It tore hungrily at fragile riverside undergrowth, ripping the earth free until it reached back to the sparse trees, trees that rooted close to the life-giving water. The savage turbulence rapaciously exposed their roots before tearing them from the earth. Uprooted, the helpless trunks were swept into the torrential chaos where, carried by the elemental flow, they further battered and smashed into the crumbling riverbanks.

I was seeing at firsthand the process of land erosion and desertification. I had wondered how the dusty land on Rancho Rajneesh had become so deeply scarred with small abysses, canyons, clefts, arroyos, and other obvious waterways, when there was no water to be seen. Now I knew. This was how deserts grew, and the speed of the process was frightening.

Nature was destroying everything that could not survive its elemental power. This was a flash flood. This is how this large ranch had come to be named the Big

Wading for the First Appointment

Muddy.

Two days after the flash flood, the river was still high. The flood damage was being repaired. Large culverts were being placed, the riverbed deepened, and the banks shored up in readiness for repairing the bridges and restoring the road. I was on the other side of the John Day River when I received word that Osho wanted a dental session.

I was delighted to be called for his first session in America. Eager to see him, and happy to use the newly-equipped dental room on the one hand, but conflicted with the realization that he might be in pain.

I radioed Ashu, Osho's original dental nurse, using a borrowed Motorola transceiver. She was working in the ranch kitchen. I told her to make her way, using the swampy back trail, to Lao Tzu House. She knew what I was referring to, and that I could not openly say that Osho wanted a dental session on the airwaves for all to hear. The local truckers could hear our messages on their CB radios, as we could pick up theirs.

I was on the other side of the river from Lao Tzu House, and the bridges had been swept away. There were no temporary bridges yet. I spoke to the two sannyasin construction workers who were busily making a new wooden bridge, telling them I needed to get to the other side. They stopped hammering, looked at each other, shrugged, grinned, looked at the river, and suggested that I wade across.

I looked into the muddy swirling waters ... mmm! But there was no other obvious way across.

Still grinning, they threw a rope across the swollen river. Their friend on the other bank tied it to a gnarled, surviving juniper tree. I tugged on the rope, testing it; I had no wish to be carried down river like an uprooted tree. Then tentatively, I waded into the water holding onto the rope above my head. Half-walking, half-hauling myself, I crossed to the other shore.

I emptied my moon boots, and attempted to squeeze the water from my heavily soaked down jacket before squelching cheerfully across country. It was at least half a mile to Lao Tzu House where Osho lived.

As I walked, I could feel the water seeping through to my underwear. Walking up Lao Tzu's sloping drive, I was very self-conscious of my bedraggled, half-drowned appearance, knowing Osho could see me through the large glass doors of his room.

Osho, unable to take his daily drives because the only road-bridge across the John Day River had been demolished by the flash flood, was simply sitting in his room. I could see the plate glass doors reflecting the newly laid grass of his garden, the many trees that had been planted, the river in the valley, and the hills on the other side. In between these reflections, through the glass darkly, I could vaguely see his outline, sitting unmoving, as still as the hills themselves. Unless one knew he was there, he could easily be missed.

Wading for the First Appointment

I entered Lao Tzu House through the mudroom of the support trailer where Osho's household staff lived. At that time, I was living in a newly erected residential trailer in the next valley. Although I was Osho's dentist, I had yet to be invited to live in his house.

Once inside, I quickly stripped down to my underwear, removing my saturated outer clothes before showering and dressing in the disposable surgical clothing I had purchased as part of the new dental protocol in the United States.

Ashu was already showered and dressed. Excitedly, we made our way along the corridor connecting the support trailer with Osho's residential trailer. Nirupa, Osho's cleaner, was meticulously washing the floor. As we passed, she gave a conspiratorial grin. She looked as excited as we were.

The tiny dental surgery behind Osho's room had a complete range of modern sophisticated United States dental instrumentation within its small dimensions. It was so packed with technology that it resembled a spaceship's cabin. I had bought this specific technical set-up of dental cabinetry because I liked the name: "The Truth System."

The dental chair was situated between two cabinets. Each had sliding glass doors and integrated technology complete with dials, tubes, knobs, handles, lights, and warning signals that either buzzed or bleeped. The overhead light, named "the Light Fantastic," was a brilliant spotlight mounted on a ceiling track. The x-ray machine was a piece of electronic wizardry that Madame Curie herself would have never recognized as bearing any relation to the pile of soot from which she had first extracted the strange stuff which glowed green in the dark, and finally killed her.

Ashu and I sat on mobile dental stools, tucked in behind the plush, green, upholstered, electronically – programmed chair. We had daily polished everything in sight, and checked our drills and gadgetry, ready for the moment we would be called for Osho's first dental session in Oregon.

Devaraj sat on the floor propped against the wall facing Osho. For him too, it was the first time in Osho's dental room. Vivek had earlier asked me if it would be a good idea for Osho's doctor to sit in on the dental sessions. She and Devaraj were good friends. I told her that his presence would be very reassuring, essential, in fact. If an emergency happened in that tiny room, it would be really difficult to move Osho to his fully-equipped medical room. The dental room was too small even for a mobile stretcher to enter.

On top of Ashu's chair side cabinet was a thick, glass, rectangular dish with a stainless steel lid. It was to hold sterilized surgical instruments; now it was empty, waiting for Ashu to fill it later.

Vivek popped her head around the door to check that we were ready. "Okay?" she queried, grinning at

Devaraj who looked a little nervous. Watching in a dental surgery affects people strangely.

"I'll be down with Osho in about thirty seconds," Vivek responded. Ashu and I sat quietly on our stools, our eyes shut, meditating before Osho came in. Everything was still and silent.

Suddenly there was a loud crack, almost an explosion!

"What was that?" I whispered, shocked. The sound had come from Ashu's direction.

Ashu looked around. There was nothing to be seen; then the glass sterile dish fell into two neat halves.

At that precise moment, the door opened and Osho silently entered, smiling, his fine hands steepled together in namaste. We three smiled back, still startled from the shock of the exploding dish. Vivek, walking behind him, closed the door.

It was Osho's first time in his new dental room. He enjoyed gadgetry of all kinds and standing there, hands on hips, he looked around. I asked if he wanted me to show him the beautiful equipment I had purchased. He nodded, and I enthusiastically demonstrated the dental machinery: the new fiber-optic drills, the computerized root canal kit, the electronic x-ray timer and self developer, the brilliant spotlight, and the relative analgesia machine. He stood, eyes shining, taking it all in.

He commented that the new dental chair was the same as our previous chair in Pune. I smiled happily that he recognized it. In Pune, he had often commented on the chair's comfort, once saying that it was the only chair where his back felt at ease. When his back pain was severe, he had asked for the dental chair to be moved into his bedroom. Moving that massively heavy hydraulic chair, I had put my own back out.

The limited space in that tiny dental cockpit made entering the dental chair a delicate manoeuvre. Lifting the chair's arm, I showed him how to slide in sideways. He got it immediately. As always, I silently marvelled at how gracefully he moved. Once seated, he slid his sandals off and Vivek took them into her care. I sat on the floor at his feet while he told me what was happening with his teeth.

I was relieved to hear there was nothing serious happening, merely some painful twinges, and he wanted his teeth checked out before they became a nuisance. I wondered to myself whether the timing of this first dental session on Rancho Rajneesh had more to do with the roads being impassable for his Rolls Royce than any dental need. And why not? Osho had a personal dentist and I was very happy to be back in my role.

While setting up his new dental room, I had discussed with Devaraj using nitrous oxide gas as a dental analgesic, explaining that "laughing gas" is commonly used for routine dentistry by English dentists. I had used it for years, finding it to be a safe and valuable resource.

Devaraj and I had researched deeply, and confirmed that nitrous oxide in dentistry was safe and without harmful side effects if used correctly. We had also unexpectedly found that nitrous oxide gas was sometimes used to relieve acute infantile asthma. It was good for dentistry and good for asthma, and that made our decision easy.

Before taking my seat I said, "Osho, in England, nitrous oxide gas mixed with oxygen is often used by dentists to make the dental session more relaxing and enjoyable. It's called laughing gas, and it helps patients not to feel minor pain or discomfort. Devaraj and I wonder if you'd like to try it."

Osho listened carefully, his eyes wide and alert. I felt that he was listening to my inner being as well as my outer words. After a small silence he nodded, saying, *"Devageet, Devaraj, do not forget my body is sensitive. Sometimes it behaves strangely with new things. You both are my medical team. I rely on you. Sometimes chemicals irritate me when they irritate nobody else. But,"* he added mischievously, *"if you want, you can try your laughing gas on me."*

I added, "The laughing gas relaxes you deeply but it doesn't send you to sleep. I'll allow it to take effect for a few minutes, and then you can tell me how you're feeling. And at the end, when I've finished the dentistry, I will tell you, and then turn off the gas and leave the machine delivering pure oxygen for a minute or two. The oxygen will flush out any remaining gas and your body will come back to normal very quickly."

Again Osho nodded and chuckled as he settled back in the chair, saying, *"You know my body, Devageet, it cannot be more relaxed. It is not possible for any man to be as relaxed as I am, but you can use your gas. I am interested to watch its effects on my body."*

I rose from the floor where I had been sitting, and squeezed my way past the dental chair to get to my stool. It really was a tight fit. Once we were all sitting in our places the tiny room was a very functional operating area, but there was very little space to move around.

I turned on the relative analgesia machine. It was a fail-safe delivery system, which meant that the oxygen level could not fall below the safe level without shutting off the machine. There was an almost imperceptible hiss as the gas started flowing.

Ashu placed the soft plastic nosepiece on Osho's nose, observing closely to see if his skin or tissues were irritated. He appeared to be perfectly at ease, as usual. Wearing the nose mask, I realized, would also keep him from being bothered by the smell of our rubber gloves, and any medications we used.

Before starting the dental work, I looked at him, not having seen him at close range since he had left Pune, except, of course, for the time I had helped rescue him from his levitated Rolls Royce. He was unchanged, timeless. Whatever the situation, he remained unperturbed.

His eyes were not quite closed. There was a glimmer beneath his slightly parted lids. His eyes were utterly still, his body silent and perfectly relaxed. He had seemingly left his body to be cared for by us. In those early days, Osho was the model dental patient, but that was to change later.

A deeply tangible silence filled the room, broken only by soft, rubbery sounds as the rebreathing bag filled with each inbreath, and then collapsed with each outbreath, and the soft hiss of the gas flowing.

We completed the dental work without any hitch.

When it was finished, I leaned over and said quietly in Osho's ear, "The dental work is over now, Osho."

I was surprised at the immediacy of his response. Without any gap or hesitation he nodded, saying, *"Now, five minutes for me. Now my work on you begins. Remember, I am in your dental chair but you are on my operating table. Now is my time."*

I looked at Ashu. Her large, green eyes were intent, absorbed in her work of gathering the used dental instruments. She momentarily met my gaze. We shared a deep rapport; it enabled us to work together without speaking. She intuitively knew my next movement; together we were as one person with four hands.

We now sat, eyes closed, meditating at Osho's side. It was always the best time of all. It was good feeling Devaraj's presence in the silence too.

The silence deepened, becoming a palpable presence, bringing an utterly delicious, inner bliss.

As I relaxed, my professional mind seemed to melt.

In that small dental room, in the middle of the Oregonian desert, we four disciples entered into a timeless, marvellous, emptiness, each of us alone, yet together in the silence we shared with our spiritual master. Osho calls it meditation. He was already there. He was always there, waiting patiently for us to enter the silence with him.

Then, very softly, I heard his voice, as if from far away. *"This is it. This is the view from the peaks. I know it well from my meditation but never before with chemicals. This gas feels very helpful. It is cooling for my lungs. I can breathe more easily. It feels good in my body."*

Though speaking, Osho was lying completely unmoving. I entered his words in my clinical notes, noting the concentration of the gases being used.

His voice was very, very faint. I wasn't sure whether anybody else had heard it. It was almost as if it was inside my head.

Moments later, he opened his eyes, smiled, and uncrossed his feet. He was ready to leave. I gave him a full minute of pure oxygen before signalling for Ashu to remove the nosemask. I leaned forward to ask if he was ready to have the chair brought back to the vertical. He nodded briefly. I pressed the buttons and the chair shuddered into action, its electric motor humming.

Once back in the sitting position, I raised the armrest, allowing Osho to slowly swing his legs to the floor. Vivek had already moved his sandals in place for him to slip into them. Resting his hand on the chair's arm, he stood upright, turned, and namasted to each of us before walking slowly and steadily from the room, his every movement soft, graceful, and strangely meaningful.

Once again, I realized that this man was qualitatively different from others. Whatever the situation, he was centred, easy and graceful. In every situation, new or familiar, he was utterly himself.

It was in moments like these that I longed for a way to convey to the world the marvel of this man. Osho's quality has nothing to do with religion or belief. He is simply, and utterly himself, always and unchangingly true, centred in his being.

In all my observations from being at his side, seeing him in many varied situations and circumstances, he is unfailingly present and alert, caring, conscious and compassionate, totally aware of all that is happening to him, and around him. Nothing seems to disturb his inner harmony and awareness.

Despite illness and injury, I have never seen Osho reduced by pain, or showing fear. Despite being highly sensitive, he never reacted impulsively to any situation, his responses were always spontaneous, conscious and intentional. All of Osho's actions seemed to emerge from a centre of monumental stillness that nothing could disturb. His movements always had the qualities of grace, silence and beauty. One had only to be near him, to observe and feel his presence, to know that here was a man in a transcendent state of consciousness.

Chapter 6

Notes of a Madman: I

Becoming Osho's Notetaker

After Osho left his private dental cabin, Devaraj, Ashu and I returned to the support trailer where Osho's household staff lived. We were exhilarated and laughing. We were always totally euphoric after an Osho dental session.

Moments later, Vivek, looking serious, entered the room where we were changing. "What were you writing on that card, Geet?" she asked. She rarely missed anything concerning Osho.

"He was saying some beautiful things, and I didn't want to forget them, so I made a note on his dental chart," I explained.

She looked doubtful. For a moment I heard the rain drumming on the roof. Until then, I hadn't realized that it was raining. I vaguely wondered if somebody had completed the roof tiling on Osho's room yet. When he had arrived on the last day of August, we hadn't had time to finish putting his trailer home together.

Vivek broke into my reverie. "I'll ask him, but it seems to me you shouldn't write down anything Osho says while he is in the dental chair."

"Don't worry," I reassured her, "it's completely

confidential. These are his clinical notes, and I keep them under lock and key. They are safe. Sometimes small things he says may turn out to be useful later. They might give an indication about how a particular treatment is affecting his body. I write everything down," I said.

Vivek, looking doubtful, went out.

She returned within a few moments saying Osho would like to see us in his room. We exchanged glances; this was very unusual.

Quickly we dressed again in our surgery clothes and followed Vivek along the corridor connecting the support trailer with Osho's own. In a single file we went down the steps, through the small cleaning room next to the dental surgery, and then across the narrow passage into Osho's large living room, which faced the hills far across the valley.

He was sitting in his high-backed chair. Asheesh, his personal chairmaker, was an Italian artisan of rare talents. Not only did he knit Osho's caps and robes, he made beautiful furniture for his room. This chair had been especially designed to support his ailing back.

Osho was looking out through the sliding glass doors as we entered. He turned and greeted us. His large eyes, soft and shining, betrayed no feeling other than simple, unconditional love.

Behind his head, I could see the sky outside was dark and clouded. Heavy rain was splashing high off the surface of the redwood veranda outside. Despite the darkness, it looked slick, red and shiny in the downpour.

His living room was very large and very empty, except for three plastic buckets strategically placed to catch water as it dripped through the ceiling. The roof tiling had clearly not been completed. Except for the buckets, the room was virtually bare. The linoleum floor covering made it seem even more so. In one corner of the room, in a little alcove I noticed a small, round, beautifully crafted dining table, with a solitary chair. Asheesh's work again.

The four of us, Vivek, Ashu, Devaraj and I, sat at Osho's feet.

Osho began by saying that Vivek had told him about me taking notes of his words. He paused momentarily and looked at his fine tapering fingers before telling us that none of the great enlightened masters from the past had written their own words. Everything we know of them has come through notes taken by their devotees.

He spoke familiarly of the sanghas of Buddha and Mahavira, their communities of disciples. He explained how the Buddha's enlightened disciples recollected his words and only wrote what they unanimously agreed were his uttered statements. These teachings were collected in what is known as the Pali Canon.

It was similar with Mahavira, only more so: Mahavira taught in silence. His enlightened disciples would gather after each silent discourse and agree together on the teachings the master had transmitted. Their collection became the scriptures of the Jains of India.

Osho emphasized to us that what we knew of the past Masters came not directly from them, but from what their disciples had passed on. These enlightened Masters from the past had raised human consciousness, but what we knew of them was from their disciples' notes.

He reminded us that we know virtually nothing of Socrates except what his disciple Plato wrote. The same is true about Jesus, and his gospel writers, Matthew, Mark, Luke and John.

The ancient Masters' immense gifts to humanity have been given to posterity through the writings of their disciples. Of the more modern masters, Osho noted that J.Krishnamurti was the only enlightened master who had written books himself; Ramakrishna was known by Vivekenanda's books, and Ramana was known from the books by the American journalist, Paul Brunton.

"It is through the writings of their devoted disciples that we know anything of the great Masters from the past." Pausing momentarily to look at me, he went on:

"You, Devageet, will be my note-taker. I will speak from the dental chair. No Buddha has ever done such a thing ... but you know me; I am a little crazy. One day these notes that you take from your dental chair will become a beautiful book. It will not be like my other books, those are from my words spoken in discourse. In my

discourses, I am speaking to the world, to the future generations of humanity. In your small Noah's Ark, Devageet, I will be speaking to just a small, intimate group of my devotees, people who love me deeply, people who are utterly in tune with me. Speaking to you, my words will possess a different quality, a new intimacy. Through these words spoken from your dental chair, people will be able to have a new glimpse of the Master. The book will be unique. No enlightened Master has ever spoken from the dental chair, and probably never will again. No Buddha has ever had his own personal dentist. Buddha himself, he had his personal physician, but not a dentist. Yes, it may appear to be a little crazy, but remember, beneath my craziness there is a sanity that can penetrate into your deepest being. My sanity is not of this world. In this insane world, a sane man looks a little mad. It has always been so."

Osho went on to say that Devaraj should edit the notes, and Ashu could type them and be Devaraj's editorial assistant. But her main function, he made clear, would be to *"be a referee for Devageet and Devaraj."* Osho chuckled as he said it.

I was puzzled when I heard these words: Devaraj and I were friends. We had never quarrelled, let alone fought. It was only three years later, when we collaborated in editing and preparing the three books that finally resulted from the dental chairside notes, that I realized how complete Osho's vision had been. He had seen clearly, three years before it happened, how Devaraj and I would argue and squabble over the placing of each punctuation mark and paragraph. He had known, and had chuckled.

He went on to say that Vivek was to take some new photos, and that she should gather some of the more intimate, older shots, showing him in his private moments: drinking tea, reading the newspaper, sleeping in his bed, photos which Vivek possessed but which hadn't yet been published. He said that this would be a beautiful and intimate book.

I gazed at this strange and wonderful man. He paid no attention to the buckets, and the plopping sound of water dripping through his ceiling. He simply and clearly told us how we should prepare the new book, explaining that it would be our work in the afternoons. In the mornings, we each had other work to do in helping Sheela to create the new commune.

Osho told us there was no need to mention our new work to others. *"When the books are ready, then people will know. Before then, it will simply make them unnecessarily curious."* He paused, smiled, then nodded very slightly to indicate that the darshan was over.

As we filed from his room I felt stunned. Things happened so fast around this man! I had just waded across the river for his first dental session in Oregon, the first in seven months. Pune seemed another world, another time. And now, I had been appointed his note taker, ready to write whatever he dictated from the dental chair.

All my life I have loved books, and nothing could have pleased me more than my new work. It wasn't work, it was a marvellous gift. I was almost delirious with joy.

The next day, at the appointed time, Ashu, Devaraj and I were sitting waiting in the tiny dental cabin. Devaraj sat on the floor facing the dental chair, his back against the wall, his long legs crossed. Ashu sat on the chair's left side, I on the right. Vivek would soon enter with Osho.

Once Osho was seated, Vivek would move his shoes to a safe place, and then come to sit next to Devaraj. After listening to what Osho had to say, I would then take my place sitting behind his head. Close at hand, balanced on the washbasin, I had a thick writing pad and several pens.

Meanwhile we sat waiting, meditating, waiting for the Master.

As usual, after a minute or two, I opened my eyes and quickly ran through the machinery functions: drills, air-water spray, suction, lights, chair. All systems were working.

The period of waiting for Osho to enter the dental room has always been a time of intense clarity for me. My mind would review everything that might be needed in the session ahead, and then it would check me out, to see what condition the dentist was in. Then, having satisfied itself, it would fall quiet, beautifully quiet. A familiar, birthday party feeling was dancing in my belly.

Into this intense silence, Vivek would jokily poke her head around the door, and ask, "Everything okay?" before invariably saying, "Osho will be down in about half a minute."

At this point, the waiting would become most acute, almost painful, exquisitely painful. The Master was about to enter; he is coming, but he is not here yet.

Osho would always enter like a gentle breeze, his feet never making a sound. Sometimes I might catch the faint sound of the door in the small neighboring room as Vivek opened it, but mostly he would simply arrive. One moment he was not there, the next moment he was standing in the doorway.

Vivek invariably held the door open for him to enter. After he had passed by, while he was namasteing us each in turn, she would close the door behind him. I would raise the arm of the dental chair enabling him to sit on the edge. There he would slip off his sandals before gently swinging his legs onto the long, contoured footrest. Replacing the armrest, I would sit at his feet, waiting until he spoke.

He might say, *"Geet, the tooth you x-rayed yesterday … it showed something?"*

And I would answer his query, talking about the tooth problem and the best treatment for it. Osho always listened carefully. Sometimes he would ask another question, other times he would simply nod; meaning, go ahead. Occasionally he would ask if there was another treatment, or what would happen if we didn't do whatever I was suggesting, or what would be the outcome if we did it differently.

Osho's queries always reflected his intelligent grasp of the dental, or any other, situation. He occasionally offered an unexpected alternative suggestion. It was more than mere lateral thinking, it was multi-dimensional. On rare occasions, he would ask Devaraj for his medical opinion on the dental situation. When he was satisfied, Osho would give a slight nod, indicating that I could begin my dental work.

While I squeezed through the narrow space between his dental chair and the cabinet, making my way to the operating stool behind him, Osho would settle his head comfortably back on the headrest. Once seated, I would tell him when I was about to press the button to electronically recline the chair. On one occasion, I hadn't warned him, and the sudden backwards movement had seemed to jolt his unprepared body.

Once he was reclining, Ashu would carefully place the gleaming white napkin around his neck. It was not an easy task because his great beard almost hid the whole bib. Hence the burning question – should the bib be over or under the beard? We agreed that the bib should cover the beard; otherwise there was no need for a napkin.

Ashu would place the soft neoprene nosemask

carefully, so as to not unduly disturb his thick moustache. At this point I would turn on the analgesia machine, adjust the mixtures of gases, and watch carefully.

There would be no sound in that tiny Noah's Ark, as Osho called our dental room, except for the soft hiss of the gas, and the rubbery sounds of the ventilator bag inflating and deflating in rhythm with Osho's breathing. Each breath he took was minimal, shallow, slow and somehow gentle. Even with his breathing he was utterly aware and caring.

The small room, already silent, would become suffused with the invisible quality of his silence; soft and deeply comforting, warming my very soul. During these precious moments next to him in the dental chair, my body seemed to dissolve, to expand into a timeless, serene emptiness.

After a few minutes, he would say quietly, *"You can begin your work now, Devageet."*

Although there was nothing urgent to do in those first dental sessions in Rancho Rajneesh, I had decided to renew his dental restorations that had been completed in India, replacing them with superior American dental materials. We had all the time we needed while the roads were impassable for his Rolls Royce.

Osho had asked Sheela to have a new road built, in addition to having the old one repaired, and to also have built a new road-bridge strong enough not to be washed away if the John Day flooded again. Osho said that a new road was needed, a road that did not cross the river and therefore could not be affected by it.

The road and bridge construction would take considerable time to complete. Meanwhile, the cold, wintry weather made working conditions outside difficult.

At the end of each dental session I would say, "The dentistry is over now, Osho." There would be a long pause, as if he was returning from far away, before he said, *"Okay, Geet, now is my time. Now my work on you begins."*

On my first day as his note taker, with my virgin writing pad open, I was ready, pen poised, waiting for Osho to begin speaking. Ashu sat with her eyes closed. Devaraj sat on the floor, wide-eyed, leaning back against the wall, with his legs stretched out almost touching the foot of the dental chair. Vivek was perched on the spare dental stool, which Osho referred to as "the horse's seat," perhaps because the stool was high, and she had to rest her feet on a circular rim of polished steel, like stirrups. It was covered in brown saddle-coloured, synthetic rawhide.

At first his words came slowly, as if from far away. The silence between the words seemed to carry as much meaning as the words themselves. His voice was very faint, a little distorted by the nose mask. I had to bend my ear close to Osho's head in order to catch what he was saying. He commented on the land of Rancho Rajneesh, the weather, the trees, his body; but above all, about the state of bliss he entered on that momentous day, March 21st, 1953, when enlightenment dissolved his ego and transformed him forever.

I was noting down cosmic gossip.

It came to me that Osho was using this unique dental situation experimentally, using nitrous oxide to see how far he could allow his consciousness to soar while still maintaining the link of verbal communication with us, his disciples. This was his constant intention when he spoke. The dental experience was yet another attempt to do the impossible, to bring the world of enlightenment into a verbal experience that might become a bridge for others to cross into the eternity he had attained.

> *Never act out of fear. Don't be worried about my body. It is okay. Don't listen to my body but to me. My body is always a little strange … it is bound to be. Once you are aware, the body starts losing its grip over the consciousness. Once you are aware, you are no more of this world. That is why the awakened one dies and is not reborn again. He cannot be born; it is impossible. He cannot have another body. This is my last body. You are fortunate to be with a person who is in the last body. I will not be again because I am Being. Once you are Being, you cannot be born again. It is Being that matters. It is Being that is eternal. Bodies come and go; Being remains.*

Bodies are born and they die. Being is neither born, nor can it die.

In that tiny Noah's Ark, he was trying new ways of communication, ways that were not possible in a large auditorium, before a large audience. The number of people, and the wide differences in their states of consciousness, affected the content of his discourse. Here, with only four of his intimate disciples, we glimpsed a mischievous, earthier, intimate side of Osho.

He showed us the man who was not only enlightened, but one who had always been a stranger in a strange world, a sane man in an insane society. Even as a child, he had battled to preserve his right to freedom and spiritual growth. His words from the dental chair gave another perspective to an already multi-dimensional man.

Paradoxically, Osho was in silence. He had entered a period of official silence when he had left India. He was giving no open discourses. In India, this man of silence often told us how he had always loved to talk. He had been the all-India debating champion while an undergraduate. One of his great joys was to take on the highest politicians in India in open debate. Political figures of the day had feared such encounters, though respecting the intellect and logical prowess of the passionate young man. Perhaps existence had contrived a way, created a dental opportunity, for him to continue expressing the truth of his sublime experience while he was in official silence. The dental sessions were not conversations. They were intimate opportunities for the Master to do his work of awakening others.

After the first session of notes, Devaraj was clearly disappointed, and a little frustrated. He could not hear his Master's words. Osho's voice, so soft and faint, could not be heard even by Ashu sitting close by his left side. Even I had to put my ear close to his mouth.

We decided that it would be better if we could tape his words, and asked Vivek to ask Osho if we could rig up a small microphone to record what he was saying. In this way, I could later check my notes against the tape, and Devaraj would be able to hear through earphones. It would immensely help his future editing.

Vivek soon brought his answer: It was fine for us to tape each session, but we should use the same tape each time. When the final note taking session was completed, we should burn the tape. When the notes had been finally transcribed and edited, we would then give them all to Sheela for publishing, keeping nothing back.

We did exactly as instructed. When the dental work was over, I would switch off the dental spotlight, bring the microphone into place – it was attached to the light – and lower it close to Osho's mouth. Nodding to Devaraj that all was in place, we would put on our earphones. Having this tape set-up meant that I could write notes without having to have my ear close to Osho's lips, and later, I could check my notes for accuracy against the taped words. The stipulation about using the same tape meant that I was kept fully stretched, dentally and mentally, having to type each day's notes before the next session was called. Sometimes there were two sessions a day, each lasting two hours or more.

It was during this time that I learned to type. I had to. Devaraj was busy with other projects, and Ashu too. It quickly became my daily task to transcribe the tapes, and the pile of papers grew quickly.

While Osho lay in the dental chair, as relaxed as any human being can be, telling beautiful stories, he started to play masterful games.

Chapter 7
Notes of a Madman: 2
The Master's Alchemical Surgery

It was after the second note-taking session, while we were sitting quietly meditating by his side, that I noticed something unusual. Osho had stopped speaking. Both of his hands were palm upwards with the index finger of each hand forming a circle with the thumb next to it. It was a traditional yoga mudra of meditation. I had never seen Osho doing it before. He was no lover of any tradition, yoga included. Alerted, I sat and watched.

While I was watching silently, the hand nearest to me was still. As I turned away to close my notebook and consider my next move, the finger-circle opened. Strange. I looked back, carefully observant, and the finger-circle closed. I noticed that when my mind was silent and meditative, Osho's right hand, the one nearest to me, was in the mudra, and when my mind was occupied with thoughts, he opened up his fingers. Occasionally, he turned his hand palm downwards and gently wagged his index finger from side to side, in silent, amused, admonishment. This was happening while he was lying still with his eyes shut, and I was sitting behind his head.

On Ashu's side, Osho was apparently doing the same with his left hand, the one nearest to her. The right and

The Master's Alchemical Surgery

left finger-circles were independently moving.

After the session, I asked Ashu if she had observed anything unusual. She too had noticed the unusual finger movements. We decided to test our theory.

That same evening, after the dental work was complete, when I saw he was placing his fingers in the mudra, I deliberately I busied my mind with a mathematical problem. Immediately the finger-circle closest to me opened up, and his index finger wagged. I silenced my mind by tuning into my breathing, and promptly his right index finger and thumb joined in a circle. I did it again and again; his fingers were immediately responsive and he was never wrong. Osho was playing masterly games.

On his other side, simultaneously, Ashu was testing his response in the same way. When she was mentally active, his finger moved in gentle admonition. When she was in meditation, his fingers formed the yoga mudra.

Osho never mentioned his silent game; he simply lay there, eyes closed, in touch with both our minds, simultaneously. I never understood how much he could see, or wanted to see, into our minds, but he certainly knew when we were thinking.

Another device Osho used during the dental note-taking sessions was to repeatedly tell me that I was being miserly with the dental gas, that I was giggling, and interrupting his speaking, that I was secretly passing notes to Ashu behind his back.

At first I was merely curious, though it quickly

became an issue for me. Day after day he would accuse me of cheating him, of not taking the notes properly, and giggling while he spoke.

"I can hear Devageet giggling … men almost never giggle. Men usually laugh or not, but they don't giggle."

"Never act out of fear. Don't be worried about my body; it is okay. Don't listen to my body, listen to me."

"Do not try to cheat me. I am such a cheat myself, you cannot cheat me."

[Notes Of A Madman: Osho]

As he made the 'accusations,' I was taking note of his words, words that appeared to be critical of me. Without there being a sound in that Noah's Ark, Osho repeatedly rebuked me, in a faint, faraway voice, for preventing him from speaking, for interfering with his relaxation, accusing me of being a coward.

"Don't be cowardly, that is the only hindrance to knowing the truth. One needs to dare to know."

[Notes Of A Madman: Osho]

It was a strange, disturbing process of attrition. Each

"critical" word dripped relentlessly into areas of my unconscious mind, areas of which I knew nothing. As water dissolves even the hardest rocks, so I felt my stoical denial that this strange process was hurting me, crumbling. Under his daily blows to my ego, I was suffering. I could not understand why he was being so apparently critical. Unconsciously, I was blaming him for the pain I was suffering from his "unjust" words.

I trusted, without clearly understanding, that his drip-drip torturous "surgery" was exposing and peeling away unseen layers from my ego citadel fortifications. In principle I knew this is the fundamental work of an enlightened Master on his disciple, but in practice I found the process excruciating. And it went on and on:

> *"But Devageet hears. I am not saying anything to him, but still he hears, and freaks out. That is the way of the coward. I call it the way of the minimum."*

[Notes Of A Madman: Osho]

My self-image as a pragmatic earthy person, not taken to bothering overmuch about unjust criticism, crumbled. I continued to write my notes, but I became emotionally affected. Osho's words dripped continuously onto my stoical defences. I felt angry with him and then guilty with myself for being angry. I got sad, and then beat myself up for being sad; after all, I was close to my

Master, and doing a job that I loved, how could I be so stupid, so unaware?

> *"Mind is always miserly, always a cheat. It cannot be otherwise. It always tries to limit, to stop, because it is always possible to control the limited."*
>
> [Books I Have Loved: Osho]

I watched as my bemused mind reeled as each masterly jab made nonsense of my usual fancy mental footwork. Since I did not know what he was referring to, I could not avoid his skillful pokes. I had put myself in the arena of the Master. I staggered emotionally from one session to the next, a deep part of me dreading what he would say next … dreading the feelings that arose as I absorbed his words. I felt outboxed; in fact I wasn't fighting, I was merely suffering, boxed in by my own inability to understand what he was doing, or why. I simply was hurting. And it got stronger.

> *"You have to listen to me, absolutely. It is a one-way affair: I say, and you listen. I order you. There is no other way. When I am working on your soul do not disturb me. So listen and don't try to say anything to me because whatever you say is bullshit!"*
>
> [Books I Have Loved: Osho]

I increasingly looked at Osho's comments as "unfair". But even when blaming him I saw that my reactions were clearly inappropriate. His uppercuts were delivered with such tenderness that I knew I was missing something important. His voice was utterly soft and caring as I went down for the count again and again, only to stagger to my feet, born aloft by the simple trust and love I had for this man. If I was feeling punished, then there had to be something in the situation that I was not seeing, a part of myself that stubbornly blamed him for causing my pain.

> *"Don't be afraid. I am always in favour of danger, and this is dangerous because you are on the very verge of consciousness. This is the time you want to stop, but this is the time I want you to go on. But you are already going back. What is there to fear? If you relax utterly and remain aware, then there are no holds, no hindrances, but gaps. The gaps are immense. You can use them as stepping stones to God."* [Books I Have Loved: Osho]

I watched my mind wriggle, trying to find a defensive position from which I could justify my negative emotions and opinions and take a stand against what he said. Sometimes I managed to feel self-righteously indignant, like any proper Englishman; other times I felt unfairly accused, like any good Jewish son doing his best, and feeling unappreciated; victims both.

> *"Now this really distracts me. I feel your bewilderment. No need to be bewildered. I am an insane man afraid of being sane again. Like an Englishman you tried hard to prevent the sneeze. Even that I understand, an Englishman tries to prevent everything possible, even a sneeze."*

[Glimpses of A Golden Childhood: Osho]

I tried to be a meditative observer as my false indifference to his painful words was systematically broken into pieces. Shattered, I caught sight of my denied feelings that lived in the darkness of my unconscious, each one a fragment of long-buried pain, and time-honoured hurt, long since locked away from the light of consciousness. Stoicism was my protection against a hurtful world, armor to protect me from ancient slings and arrows.

> *The other day, Devageet, I saw you were a little hurt again because I called you a fool. Please try to understand the language of a madman. Fool simply means the simple, the childlike, the innocent. That is why the other day I called you a fool, with great love. I can only call someone a fool when I love them. When I call you a fool, rejoice! Rejoice totally, only then you will begin to understand. The fool is available, ready, ready*

> *to change. The idiot is hard, very hard. An idiot's head is covered with steel, nothing can penetrate him. I can hear the giggle of the fool. I called you the fool, and still you are nice to me. And I will go on calling you the fool, because I want to kill the fool, to crush the fool completely. I want you to be without it."*

[Glimpses of A Golden Childhood: Osho]

Being close to the Master is being on his operating table. He had warned me. As a master-surgeon, his work is subtle, his touch sure. There can be no anaesthetic because the only way for unconscious wounds to heal is to bring them into the light of conscious awareness; and to feel them. These ancient wounds hidden behind walls of ancient denial served to continuously deaden me to reality, sitting between me and my life, filtering, censoring each event for potential pain. To heal my core wounds, I needed to remain conscious, to see, feel and understand each exposure, each layer of my wounded psyche that my Master was exquisitely laying bare and excising.

> *"I have not shouted for twenty-five years, but for your sake I say, shut up! Not for you, but the fool within you. If you bug me I can be terrible. It is I who will have the last laugh."*

[Glimpses of A Golden Childhood: Osho]

His work is delicate, and easy to misunderstand. He can only operate within an atmosphere of complete trust. He was trusting me to understand what he was doing, and why. My trust enabled me to make the effort to put aside my instinctive reactive pain and its attendant emotions and search for the motive behind Osho's apparently unjust words. I was learning to replace fear with awareness, and it took all my trust.

He and I both knew that at any time I could withdraw my consent to this strange process. That was my intrinsic freedom, and Osho would never interfere with it. But as the abrasive process went on, I realized that my trust, though sincere, had limits. My trust was carrying old wounds from past encounters during my early life. My ego's protective strategies were being exposed as I sought out the possible motives for my Master's "criticisms."

Daily, the mental patterns and emotional reactions that buttressed my ego were systematically and surgically exposed by his comments. I was beginning to see blind spots in my psyche. What had been hidden was emerging from the mist of confusion. What had been unconscious was now being dragged screaming and complaining into the light of awareness.

"I could not sleep the whole night. I think the cause was that I was a little too hard on Devageet. Yes, I can be very hard. I am not hard but I can be very hard, particularly at certain moments

when I see a possibility of some opening in you. Then I really hit! Not with a small hammer, with a sledgehammer. When one has to hit, why choose a small hammer? Be finished with a single hit.

The moment I left the room I saw you looking a little sad. Whatsoever the reasons for your sadness, I had, in some way, deepened the darkness in you. And I am here to enlighten you, not to endarken you. I was just a little concerned about Devageet, feeling as if I had hurt him. Perhaps I had done it ... perhaps it was needed ... but remember not to get disturbed if I am hard."

[Glimpses of A Golden Childhood: Osho]

His loving barbs transformed the dental cabin into a strange laboratory, with my skull becoming the crucible for his alchemy of love. The friction between his words and my ego-mind brought an intense heat, a fire of transmutation that forced the detritus of my early life conditioning to be burned away under the dual catalysts of trust and emerging awareness.

"Poor Devageet, no matter how hard I hit him he never takes revenge. So good. Anybody, and when I say anybody, I mean Moses, Jesus, Buddha, would be jealous of me. Gautam the

> *Buddha had his own personal physician, but no Buddha has ever had his own personal dentist. They were certainly not so fortunate. At least nobody had a Devageet with them, that much is absolutely certain."*
>
> *[Glimpses of A Golden Childhood: Osho]*

I could feel how his words were polarizing my trust in him as my Master, setting it against my long-held negative beliefs and attitudes that had arisen from being born Jewish on the eve of World War Two: Trust nobody. Life is a battle. Take care of yourself because nobody else will. He stoked the alchemical fire relentlessly. In each dental session he raised the heat. The heat brought some light. I could see what had long been hidden. The heat cauterised wounds I had long denied.

> *"And poor Devageet. I can still hear his giggles. My God! Can no chemistry at least prevent me from hearing the giggles?*
>
> *But I love and I trust Jews. Just look in this Noah's Ark: there are two and a half Jews. I am a perfect Jew without any hesitation. Devageet is not a perfect Jew, just a Jew. Devaraj is partially a Jew and doing his best to hide it, but that only makes it more Jewish."*
>
> *[Glimpses of A Golden Childhood: Osho]*

Osho carefully balanced my acceptance and trust of him against my ego boundaries of pain and anger. If he overstepped the limits, then my ego would explode into angry reaction. Not that my anger would affect him, but he knew it would cut short the operation and alter the outcome of this spiritual surgery.

My trust, freely and sincerely given, was being tested down to its bedrock as my ego felt itself deliberately under attack. My ego insisted it was protecting me; hadn't it always protected me, since childhood? Its ways and strategies were rooted in ancient conflicts and agonies, each with its own apparent validity, yet none of them were able to stand the metamorphic fire with which Osho was torching them.

Osho's drip-drip derision was forcing me to question him. Did he really want to hurt me? My mind shouted, "Why is he doing this to you?" Of course not, whispered my heart. He is not doing it *to* you, but *for* you: Feel his love. Be grateful.

> *"I just had a golden experience, the feeling of a disciple so lovingly working on his Master's body. I am still out of breath because of it, and it reminds me of my golden childhood…"*

[Glimpses of A Golden Childhood: Osho]

So why am I feeling so bloody and torn, demanded my mind, as it was taken beyond its limits of understanding into the heart's vastness of trust. My heart could recognise the unconditional love behind my Master's words, and surrendered happily. My heart did not care what Osho did; it trusted him more deeply than it trusted my poor old conditioned mind. I trusted him more than I trusted my "self."

> *Devageet, I have been too hard on you this morning. I will not say anything about it, only this much; with whomsoever I love, I forget that I have to behave. Then I start doing or saying things which are okay if I am alone ... and that's what love is, to be with someone as if one were alone. But sometimes it can be a little hard on the other person.*
>
> *I can always say 'sorry,' but it is so formal. And when I hit, and I hit often, I hit hard. I remind you, in the future too, I will be hard, perhaps harder, on you. That is my way of being loving.*
>
> *I hope you will understand – if not today, then tomorrow, or perhaps the day after tomorrow. More than that I cannot say because at least for these two days I am booked, I am going to be here.*
>
> *[Glimpses of A Golden Childhood: Osho]*

And he went on, taking me deeper and deeper, to my core

Devageet, you are not the only Jew here. Remember you are not in a hurry. I am in a hurry; my bladder is hurting! So please, Devageet, you would have been such a good nagging wife. Really! I mean it. Just find a nice boy and go on honeymoon...

[Glimpses of A Golden Childhood: Osho]

I heard Osho accuse me of being a nagging, Jewish housewife, constantly interrupting him while he was talking. He had been regularly referring to me as a fool. As he spoke I was writing his excruciating words as fast as my fingers could manage. It became suddenly too much. As he left the session, as I looked into his smiling, warm eyes, something snapped.

In the empty dental room, I sat on my operating stool, head in hands, my frustrated anguish turning to tears, wondering what I was doing to prompt this continual barrage of derision. Though his words were gently spoken, they had finally penetrated the concrete bunker of my main ego fortifications.

When Osho had started to make hurtful comments, I had asked Vivek what she thought he was referring to when he repeatedly said I was interrupting, when all I was doing was noting his words. Sitting where she did,

Vivek couldn't actually hear what he said. Moreover, she appeared less than interested in my question; bored in fact, saying in an offhand way that Osho must be referring to my chattering mind getting in the way of my note taking; adding somewhat maliciously, perhaps I was too unconscious to notice how much interference my mind was making.

I looked at what she said from all angles. Each one hurt.

She might well have been right, but for the life of me I could not relate to Osho's comments about my mental state. Often, his most punishing words came when I was completely absorbed in writing furiously, a task which occupied me totally, physically and mentally, a task that I loved. Writing his notes left me no time for thinking. So what was he referring to?

When I tried to discuss my confusion with Devaraj, he had simply shrugged. I gathered that he felt it was not important enough to worry about; which was fine for him, but it was happening to me.

I came to realize that I desperately wanted Osho's approval; and instead, I was getting the opposite. It brought up my childhood feelings of insecurity, abandonment and rejection, unworthiness and pain. I tried, ineffectually, to be angry with Osho, but it was the seeming unfairness that had finally gotten to me.

In speaking with Ashu, hoping for solace more than a solution, I felt that she was subtly grateful that it was me on the sharp end of Osho's barbs, and not her. I noticed how she giggled delightedly when he told me that I was a nagging wife.

Now, years later, it is wryly funny, though at the time I felt like a grape being squashed beneath my Master's foot so that he could extract my best possible juice. Retrospectively, I can see that my pain resulted from being identified with being the grape skin; identifying with the outer, oblivious to the inner juice.

Occasionally I could peer over the top of my prickly, ready-to-be-offended, hair-triggered ego. But my ego was a tough, obstinate, old street fighter, programmed for survival at all costs, seeing every pain as vindication of its belief that the world is cruel. My awareness had yet to be polished into reflective clarity and could not yet see the point of my master's cutting words. At this stage, I could only feel the pain of his scalpel exposing and agonisingly stripping the skin from my unconscious wounds. I could not see he was healing them.

That day, in desperate tears, I wrote him a letter:

Beloved Osho,
  Here I am, sitting in the Noah's Ark, weeping and wondering what to do. When you are here, and I am empty of everything except your words and presence pouring through me, it is the greatest fulfilment I have known. Then you hit – from nowhere!

You tell me I am giggling, when, for example this morning, I suppressed a sneeze. Other days, sighs escape my lips; what to do? I sigh when you are close. Again, you tell me that I am giggling. When you accuse me of deceiving you by only pretending to write your notes it is too much!

I love writing these notes beyond any other thing in my life. The writing of them is a pleasure, a gift beyond any possibility my mind may have conceived.

You have called me a fool, and that is obviously so, perhaps never more than now, but I am your fool through and through. I have never cheated you, betrayed you, never giggled or whispered to deceive you, and I always give you the maximum, and the pain from the hit is not from the blow but from the apparent injustice of it.

Beloved Osho, I am your fool and never more than at this moment.

I love you,

Devageet

P.S. Thank you for destroying me, it seems to allow me to love you even more deeply.

P.P.S. Please keep up the good work forever.

I gave the letter to Vivek to deliver to Osho, though normally, on the ranch, every letter to Osho went through

Sheela. But Vivek accepted it.

Osho answered my letter in the next dental session. His answer left my mind as puzzled as before, but my heart understood enough for it to become still and content.

> *I knew Devageet would cry and weep. I knew. How did I know even before he had written to me? Even if he hadn't written to me, I would have known. I know my people. I know those who love me whether they say it or not. And what really touched me were his words, "You can hit me as much as you want, that does not hurt; what hurts is that when I am not giggling you say, 'Devageet don't try to deceive me.'" "This hurts. It is the apparent injustice of it that hurts." The words 'apparent injustice' exactly show his heart. He knows it is only apparent, but it certainly looks unjust. Naturally he is taken aback. And poor Devageet is just taking his notes.*
>
> *Devageet, your letter was beautiful, and you cried. I feel happy about it. Anything authentic is helpful on the way, and nothing can be as authentic as tears. Yes, there are professional weepers, but they have to use tricks. If you are sad, tears come. If tears come, for any reason, even chemical tears – let us call them artificial*

tears – then too, just because of an instinctive heritage you will feel sad.

Tears out of love are the most precious experience.

You cried, and I am happy because you could have been angry, but you were not; you cried, that is as it should be.

But remember, I will go on doing the same again and again: I have to do my work. It has to be 'apparently unjust.' But you mentioned the word 'apparent.' That's enough to satisfy me that although it hurts, you understand my love.

Let me repeat again and again so that you do not forget: I will do it again and again!

I simply go on hitting, this side and that. Because you both happen to be on either side, naturally, you get most of the hits. This has always been my way; those who are nearest to me have been hit the most, but they have also grown. They have become more integrated with each hit they absorbed.

Either they ran away or they had to grow. Do or die. If you do – that's what I mean by integration, or crystallization – only then do you live.

The letter was beautiful in many senses.

Devageet says in his letter, "Osho I trust you."

I know. There is no question about it – otherwise why should I hit you so much? And remember, once I trust someone I never mistrust them. It does not matter what that person does to me. My trust remains whatever the person does.

Trust is always unconditional. I know your love, and I trust you all otherwise this work would not have been given to you. But remember, that does not mean I will change in any way. Letter or no letter, P.S. or no P.P.S. I am going to remain the same.

You know your work, and I know my work, and it is far more difficult. It is not only drilling, it is drilling without anaesthesia, not even a painkiller. It is not only drilling into your teeth it is drilling into your very being. It hurts, it really hurts.

Forgive me, but never ask me to change my

strategies. And in your letter you have not asked either. I am just saying it for the benefit of the others present."

[Glimpses of A Golden Childhood: Osho]

After Osho's answer, I rarely had a problem when he threw the odd "insult" at me. Instead, I tried to look carefully into its context, trying to get the point instead of feeling merely pricked.

I tried to receive each hit from him as a love bolt, as part of the mystery of Osho's work. I had at least come to recognise that I only felt hurt when he unearthed a nodule of ancient pain hidden in my unconscious mind. Ouch! meant he had found the target. This expert marksman was sniping at my ego. And, hadn't he said he hits hardest at those who are closest to him? That gave a little salve to my bruises.

The Master's Alchemical Surgery

Osho with a small group of disciples in the Lao Tzu garden 1974

The Master's Alchemical Surgery

Osho on the veranda of Lao Tzu house 1974

Chapter 8
Notes of a Madman: 3
My Days Were Numbered

At the beginning of the sixth note-taking session, Osho quietly announced that series one had now been completed, and series two was about to begin. The new series was centred around the ancient Tibetan mantra, *Om Mani Padme Hum*, which he told us is a statement of the living heart of the universe, the soundless sound of existence, the heartbeat of the Absolute. Of these talks he said, *"I will continue to speak on this most ancient of all mantras, Om Mani Padme Hum, until your concrete skull is broken, Devageet, until it has penetrated into your deepest unconscious."*

Deep inside something trembled. My name, Devageet, has the same meaning as this mantra. Giving me my sannyas name, in 1976, Osho had spoken of Om Mane Padme Hum as being the essence of all authentic religious experience.

Osho's dictated words were not comments on the traditional meaning of the mantra but I felt them to be utterances from the same inner state of consciousness that had originally inspired the ancient seers of Tibet. Osho spoke from the core-truth of his own mystic experience. His words were transmitting the living pulse of existence itself: Om Mani Padme Hum.

Six sessions later, he just as suddenly announced the start of the third series of notes. It was to be a journey in which he recalled many of the inspirational books he had enjoyed throughout his lifetime.

Osho was a lifelong bibliophile. As a student, he had starved in order to buy books of his choice. Throughout his life he had always possessed a large collection of fine books, and in Pune, his library was vast; in fact, his whole house was one large library.

From the dental chair in deepest Oregon, Osho spoke of those rare books whose words echoed the eternal essence of the mystery of life that is hidden in all forms, the formless mystery into which he had dissolved when he became enlightened. I felt that he was transmitting that same mystery as I wrote his notes from the dental chair.

Osho spoke of authors across the spectrum of truth from Tolstoy to Richard Bach, taking in Wittgenstein and Madame Blah-Blah Blavatsky along the way: Hassids, Zen Masters, Sufis, mystics of all ages, shapes and sizes were paraded before us, each one nobly attempting to express the inexpressible, and relishing the challenge of the impossible. Osho, by referring to their written work, was offering them recognition for their magnificent efforts.

At the opening of the series, he had declared that he wanted to talk about the same number of books as the years of his life. He was fifty-one years old at that time. He said he would speak on about ten books per session. His sense of numbers being famously erratic, he asked me to help him stay on track.

Starting the new series, Osho numbered each volume as he went along. After volume number three he asked, *"Devageet, what number are we on now?"*

I answered, "Number four, Osho."

"Right," he replied. *"Number five."*

He had leapt to number five. I had answered his question by telling him the number of the next book, but he had jumped ahead. I was confused. He was already speaking, so I continued to write my notes. But I was worried because we had no volume number four.

Three volumes later he asked, *"Devageet, what is the number now?"*

What could I do to rectify the number confusion? We were actually on volume number six, but due to Osho's unexpected leap ahead, we were referring to it as number seven. I decided to try and bring the numbers back on track. "The last book was number six, Osho."

"Good," he replied. *"Number six,"* And he continued to speak. Now I was doubly confused: we had no number four, and two number sixes, and soon we would have two number sevens. I decided to try and correct the numbers later while I was editing the day's notes.

The next day the same thing happened. Whatever number I told him, Osho would either go forward or backward, or sometimes simply stay on the same number.

My Days Were Numbered

In my room, as I tried to salvage my lost sanity from the mess of numbers, I was never certain whether I had it right or not.

In each session, after the first two or three volumes, he would ask, *"Devageet, what number book are we on now?"* If the last book had been number three, I would answer, "Number four, Osho,"

I had meant that the next book should have been number four but perhaps he assumed I had been speaking of the last book, not the next. This meant that every day number four was missed.

Each time he asked what number we were now on I would try to recover the lost numbering by doing it the other way around. For instance, if the last book had been number eight, I would say, "This book is number eight, Osho," expecting him to continue at number nine. But he didn't. He would then say, *"Okay, number eight."* We would now have two number eights and no number four. In addition to taking the notes, which needed all my attention, in my mind I would be trying to find a way to answer his next query about the numbers. I never worked it out. If I went one way, he went the other. If I went down, he went up.

In one particular session, we had two number fours, three number sixes, and a couple of number nines. Instead of speaking on ten books he had spoken on fourteen, or was it thirteen? It looked like a simple problem, but I never managed to solve it. After a time I gave up trying to hold the numbers down, convincing myself that since Osho was incompatible with mathematics there was nothing I could do. Perhaps I had caught his numeric disease. I consoled myself by deciding to fix the numbers when the notes were being written into manuscript form.

One day Osho asked me how many books he had spoken about thus far into the series. I had no idea. On hearing my muttered admission of ignorance, he said, *"Devageet, I am the drunkard here, not you. You should be at least able to count to ten. I cannot count beyond three before losing the thread. I am relying on you to keep track."* I told him, miserably, that I would read through all the notes and have the answer ready for the next session. He simply chuckled.

In searching through my pile of notes I found to my horror that we had overshot the birthday target. We had actually covered sixty-four books. On telling Osho the news, he was silent for a long moment before deciding to add a postscript. He said he would change his original intention and speak instead on two volumes for each year of his life, because there were so many authors clamoring to get onto his list. Presumably they were clamoring from the other side of the Great Divide. As he was speaking it often felt as if he was in direct touch with the dead authors.

The postscript with its additional number of books only gave more scope for my numerical nightmare. Each session, he would innocently pull the strings and all the numbers danced out of any semblance of order. I could only watch helplessly.

Inevitably, after a few sessions, he would ask the question I had been dreading, *"How many books have we spoken about all together, Devageet?"*

Each time I was flummoxed, mumbling that I would have to again check through my notes, knowing, even as I spoke, that we were probably over the target once more.

And so it was.

On hearing that we had overshot the second target by a dozen or more books, Osho cheerfully added a second postscript, saying, *"Okay, make it three books for every year of my life."*

But the second postscript meant only that I had to ride my numerical nightmare yet again. Nothing was solved. My numbers were always wrong, utterly and continually wrong, and getting more so with each session. I abandoned hope of ever reining them back into the corral of order. Without hope for any numerical solution, I relaxed.

The book series ended when Osho dedicated the last volume to the memory of Alan Watts, an American who, according to Osho, could have attained to enlightenment if only he had taken the opportunity to be with an enlightened Master. Instead, Alan Watts had died a drunk, a brilliant lush whose mystic insights and clarity of exposition opened up Eastern philosophies and religions to Western seekers in the second half of the twentieth century.

It was a fascinating series of talks, but I breathed a sigh of relief when the question of numbers vanished. Surveying the problem afterwards, feeling my ineptitude, I reminded myself that Osho often said in the sessions, *"Devageet, go beyond numbers."* A cryptic remark that seemed to grow until it appeared to apply to almost everything in my life.

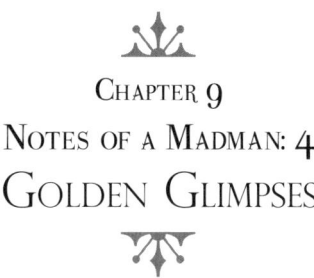

Chapter 9
Notes of a Madman: 4
Golden Glimpses

The fourth series of notes from the dental chair proved to be the last. It was about Osho's childhood:

Everybody talks of his golden childhood, but rarely, very rarely, is it true. Mostly it is a lie. But so many people are telling the same lie that nobody detects it. Even poets go on singing songs of their golden childhood – Wordsworth for example, not a worthless fellow at all – but a golden childhood is extremely rare, for the simple reason: where can you find it?

Osho told stories of his early years that he had never revealed before. He had us laughing, sometimes crying, but mostly stunned at his sheer audacity as a child. His words took us back fifty years, to a time and context no longer existing in India.

In remembering details of childhood incidents with his teachers, parents, family and friends, told in the strange intimacy of his private dental cabin in an Oregonian desert, Osho didn't merely recall his early years, he was reliving them.

While telling a hilarious story of a man losing his

trousers, Osho was roaring with laughter. His laughter was infectious. I could barely hold my pen, and Devaraj needed to clutch tightly to his earphones. Ashu giggled so hard she almost slipped from her stool. I'd never seen him so extraordinarily ordinary. His uproarious enjoyment dissolved any barriers of formality.

When he told us of being eight years old, sitting in a creaking bullock cart, holding the head of his beloved dying grandfather in his lap, we cried. When his best friend died in the river's swollen floodwaters, we were shaken. When he spoke of the two enlightened Masters who had recognized and nurtured his spiritual potential, we were entranced.

His stories about nailing ghosts to trees, of putting a large snake beneath his teacher's chair, of jumping into the dangerous whirlpool to learn the truth of let-go, showed us the immense depths of trust that had brought him to his enlightenment. We sat in grateful awe. Among his many attributes, this man Osho is a master storyteller.

And then, suddenly, after two months, Osho stopped speaking as suddenly as he had started. The notes from the dental chair ended. Not with any particular event, nor had his childhood been fully travelled. He simply ended with the words: *"And Devageet, it is beautiful, but enough. Devaraj, help him. Ashu, do your best. I would love to continue but time has gone. One has to withdraw somewhere. Stop!"*

I continued the mammoth task of typing and editing

the huge pile of notes into readable form. Devaraj was happy to leave the donkeywork to me, until the day when Osho asked him how the book was going. He didn't know.

Devaraj came galloping into our small, shared bedroom, saying urgently, "Geet, he's asking for the book! Is it nearly ready? What can I tell him?" I was irritated. Until this moment Raj had shown little interest in the work of editing the notes. I said, "Well, I'm ploughing through them. I have almost completed the first edit."

He interrupted brusquely saying, "Let me see what you've done. I have to be able to tell Osho tonight when I give him his medicines." He took a sheaf of notes and began to read. After a few minutes he said, "Geet, I don't remember Osho saying this, or this or this. Where are the originals?"

Thus began a painstaking review of all the notes. Devaraj and I were often at loggerheads over Osho's exact meaning. We argued and fought over every full stop and comma … just as Osho had predicted two years previously, with Ashu often acting as the referee.

The raw material included pages of comments about the ranch, about America, and some highly personal asides, and after many weeks of editing, we finally hammered out three recognizable books. While we edited madly, Osho would periodically insert a shaft of urgency by asking Devaraj about the book's progress.

After having been told that the first draft was complete, Osho sent word asking if there were any points that needed clarification. There were, especially around certain dates and times. He suggested that we write the queries down as questions, and he would set up another, final, session to give us the answers we needed.

One particular query concerned the date of the death of Magga Baba, one of the enlightened men who had befriended Osho as a child. Our notes showed him dying in three different places, at different times. Each narrative contained a touching poignancy, but we wanted to get it right.

In the ensuing session supposed to answer our queries and settle our confusion, Osho gave us a fourth version of the death of Magga Baba. Far from being clearer, we now had an additional touching version. Each story of the death told the tale from a different perspective, giving another insight into the unique relationship between the older man and the boy-Buddha. It was inconceivable to interrupt Osho while he was speaking. We simply took the new notes back and transcribed the newest version of the death of Magga Baba.

But how to choose from them all which one was true?

We sent a letter to Osho, telling of our difficulty. He replied saying that he had said all there was to say about the death of Magga Baba. All the versions were true, and we should use our own intelligence to select the final version.

Stunned, I surveyed the difference between the

vastness of truth and the narrowness of factuality. Truth was a whole world unto itself, and facts were small railway tracks that attempted to cross it. Osho is a man of truth, as was Magga Baba, and mere words could never contain the truth of what happened between them. Maybe all factuality, when scrutinized, dissolves into versions, tracks, of varying validity depending on the context at the time, and the needs of the questioner to arrive at a conclusion. Truth remains beyond. The lesson for me was to open my capacity to listen in order to hear the silent centre of truth within the cyclone of facts.

It took three years to type and edit the notes from the dental chair. Finally, at the end of 1984, they were ready for publication. Osho did not read them. He had told us he never read any of his books. He trusted us.

We sent him a message saying the book had become three volumes, and they were completed except for their titles. He replied, asking Raj and I to send him a list of suggested titles from which he would choose.

We pondered and brainstormed, making and discarding titles by the score. Our tiny room was littered with paper. Vivek, who had never liked the idea of the notes from the outset, walked out of our room one day muttering, "Nobody's going to read this book. It's just the bloody notes of a madman."

Looking at each other, Raj and I quickly wrote her words at the top of our list: Notes of a Madman, as a suggested title for the first volume. Of course Osho chose it.

The second volume to emerge from the notes, has the title, "Books I Have Loved", must surely be the only volume by an enlightened Master speaking of the writings of poets and mystics whose vision of truth he recognized and appreciated. This volume is a tribute to their poetic insights being as one with Osho's personal experience of eternity.

"Glimpses of a Golden Childhood", the third volume, became an instant bestseller in the sannyas world and beyond. As a book it is simply unique: it is a Buddha telling something of his budding.

My heart is beating fast as I remember those wonderfully mad, often excruciating, but never less than magnificent days in the tiny dental "Noah's Ark" on Rancho Rajneesh. I smile knowing this was the only time in the whole history of mankind when a living Buddha has spoken from the dental chair: his personal dental chair at that.

Being Osho's note taker was a timeless, mind-shattering, alchemical experience which stays bright and alive in my memory, a star shining from a clear night sky guiding me home.

Chapter 10
The Fearful Specialist

It was 1984, Rajneeshpuram, Oregon: A time of increasing conflict between the developing sannyasin community of Rajneeshpuram, and the people of the state of Oregon. There was a statewide media campaign orchestrated in support of the state government versus the city of Rajneeshpuram. The political strategy was simple: to use the courts to provide a legal solution to what was essentially a political decision, to get Osho and his people out of the state of Oregon.

The city of Rajneeshpuram – the city of Osho – had been legally incorporated. But that had happened before anti-Osho hysteria had peaked into a vote-catching, and politically valuable topic of major interest. Determined attempts were being made to declare the city of Rajneeshpuram illegal, and part of the method employed by the state-suppliant media was to marginalize the citizens of the new city.

The media campaign against the city denigrated the way of life and the beliefs of the people of Rajneeshpuram, and generally demeaned the community of sannyasins. The press supported the strategy by daily publishing hate-filled letters and biased articles. The Thousand Friends of Oregon, a powerful land use-lobby whose founder members were lawyers with political ambitions, made it their avowed intention to destroy Rancho Rajneesh, and remove Osho and his people from the state.

Sannyasins were depicted as a gun-crazy bunch of new-age religious zealots who wanted to take over the state of Oregon by fair means or foul. Hysteria was raised to fever pitch. Osho was named by Time magazine as the media person of the year because his name sold more papers than any other.

David Frohnmeyer, Oregon's Attorney General, was an example of the top-end complicity of Oregon state officials who attempted to use United States law to provide a political solution to the problem of removing Osho from United States soil. The state governor, Vic Attiyeh, further escalated the public controversy around Rajneeshpuram by announcing on a popular TV chat show, "Hello America," that the City of Rajneeshpuram was "illegal" because it contravened the American constitution that requires the separation of church and state.

He ignored the fact that many other parts of the United States have communities with a single, dominant religious group, including the Mormon population of Salt Lake City, the Baptist strongholds of Alabama, Georgia, Tennessee and Mississippi, and the Catholics of Louisiana. More importantly, he omitted mentioning that the Wasco County Oregon court had examined the original application to incorporate the city of Rajneeshpuram and had approved it. The city was legal in the eyes of the law, but the state governor openly declared otherwise.

The immediate effect of his statement was to create fear among the creditors of Rajneeshpuram, making it difficult for Osho's people to conduct normal trading with their neighbors. The city was in the middle of a neglected, semi-desert region, miles from other towns, and its residents were largely dependent on local suppliers for their general needs.

Local stores were meanwhile doing a roaring trade selling t-shirts with Osho's head outlined in the cross-hairs of a rifle-sight, accompanied with the words, "Better Dead Than Red," referring to the red clothing Osho's people wore.

It was during this time of heated public controversy that Osho began to have sporadic toothaches. I could not find any clinical cause. Discussing the elusive pain with my dental colleague, Anutosh, brought no clear explanation. I asked Osho if we should invite a specialist from Portland. He agreed.

This was a delicate affair for several reasons, primarily because the intense public hostility to the sannyasin community made it unlikely that any specialist of repute would want to make the one hundred and twenty-mile round trip into the heart of a "cultist" community in the wilderness. Secondly, because I was a dental outlaw.

I was performing dentistry on Osho without an Oregon state license. The fact that my one and only patient was Osho did not alter the fact that I was a dental persona non grata, a dental Robin Hood. This meant that I could not present myself to the visiting specialist as Osho's personal dental practitioner.

We decided to present Anutosh, a Canadian licensed to practise in Oregon, as Osho's dentist, and I would present myself as his former Indian dentist and his current dental advisor. The plan was workable but presented logistical problems. Osho's tiny dental room would need to accommodate three extra people: the specialist, his nursing assistant, and Anutosh. In addition, Anutosh would need to appear to be familiar with the room, with Osho, and with the current dental problem.

On the day of the specialist's appointment we were semi-rehearsed and almost prepared. The specialist and his dental nurse were escorted to the Lao Tzu support trailer by security staff.

When they arrived to an enthusiastic greeting with tea and cake, they already looked pale and shaken by the long drive and the subsequent ordeal of journeying into the heartland of Oregon's public enemy number one. Because of daily threats of violence by gun-happy locals, the city had set up a series of police checkpoints along the road into Rajneeshpuram from Antelope. The specialist was nervous, while his dental assistant, a buxom young blonde, was cheerful, friendly and innocently curious.

When asked if they would like to shower and refresh themselves after their tiring journey, the young woman happily took the opportunity, while her boss looked even more frightened and suspicious. We assured him that we had two separate fully equipped bathrooms, in case he thought we were suggesting he and his nurse should bathe together. He declined gruffly.

During the teatime conversation, the specialist had asked our respective roles, and Ashu and Anutosh played their roles well, while Devaraj and I kept our English accents well to the rear, although Devaraj was licensed to practise as a physician in Oregon. We wanted to keep any disturbing factors to a minimum.

Before our appointed time with Osho, Devaraj, Ashu, Anutosh and I showered and outfitted ourselves in the usual full surgical gear. Our dental guests were similarly clothed. We walked in a singlefile along the corridor linking the support trailer with Osho's residential trailer, into the tiny dental room.

When we had asked the specialist to remove his shoes on entering the house trailer, it had provided yet another emotional hiccup. Seeing that everybody else was shoeless, and taking the offered house slippers had mollified him somewhat. Now, seeing us all kitted up with surgical bootees, he became more relaxed. For the specialist, this was just a routine dental examination, and these complex surgical precautions must have seemed a little excessive. Devaraj had carefully explained Osho's extreme allergic sensitivity, but that too had added to the aura of strangeness.

On entering, the specialist, seeing the empty chair, had asked, "Where's the patient?" I had replied that he would be brought down in a few minutes. In normal medicine, it is the patient who waits, not the specialist. This additional irregularity on top of the others miffed him even more.

In the tiny dental cabin, it was a very tight squeeze to fit everybody in. I could see the specialist's emotional tolerance point was reaching its limit. We tried to keep things light with funny banter.

In that crowded room, Vivek suddenly opened the connecting door to announce that Osho would be down in half a minute. Seeing the room crowded with surgically shrouded figures her eyes widened, but thankfully Devaraj joked with her, and her spontaneous distaste of the situation was put on hold. She knew we needed the specialist's opinion but she was fiercely protective of Osho's comfort.

We stood silently waiting for our patient. In the silence the nervous tension mounted.

Moments later, the door opened and Osho stood on the threshold. He greeted us with his hands together in smiling namaste. We replied in kind, while the specialist and his nurse looked on, baffled at these strange rituals. I noticed that Osho's full-length robe and hat had taken the specialist by surprise.

I led Osho into the dental chair. He sat on the edge while Vivek removed his sandals and placed them carefully

The Fearful Specialist

out of harm's way. He swung his legs up onto the extended footrest and leaned back in the chair. Anutosh introduced the specialist, but Osho, never having spoken to Anutosh before, could not fully understand his Canadian accent. I repeated his words, and Osho greeted the specialist with a welcoming smile. I stepped back, alert for whatever came next.

The specialist, clearly happy at last to have the initiative, questioned Osho about the frequency and duration of the pain. He spoke quickly, probably out of his nervousness in this strange situation. Osho looked at him, before asking me, *"What is he saying Geet?"*

I translated, and that awkward moment passed into another. The specialist could not understand Osho's reply. "Is he speaking English?" he asked brusquely. I nodded and suggested that I act as interpreter. Clearly, Oregon and Pune could not communicate.

The specialist asked Osho to open his mouth, and then proceeded to vigorously strike each tooth. In the silence each tap sounded like a blow. I could feel Osho's whole body react to the unusual force. I quietly asked the specialist if he could hit the teeth with less force, mentioning that Osho's sensitivity was great enough for even a minimal tap to evoke the sought-after pain.

I thought the specialist was going to explode. His face became red while major blood vessels in his neck bulged alarmingly. I added quickly, "I am not criticizing your method but you have probably not treated an

The Fearful Specialist

enlightened man before. His body is extremely sensitive."

He did not reply to my words but changed his method. He asked his nurse for the tooth-vitality tester, a small electrical device that transmits an electrical current into the tooth. If the nerve is dead, the pain reaction is less than if the tooth is alive and well.

She handed her chief the small hand-held device. He switched it on, checking there was current flowing. A small light glowed red. He put it into Osho's mouth and pressed the switch ... no light. Irritated, he withdrew the vitality tester from Osho's mouth and tested it again; the light glowed red. He placed it back inside ... the light failed to shine.

The specialist was beginning to lose his composure. He barked at his dental nurse, "Did you put new batteries in this thing?"

She nodded, "Yes, doctor. I always put in new batteries as a routine."

"Well they must be faulty! Replace them!" His words were curt, snappish, indicating his inner turmoil. She left the room with Devaraj.

Osho said quietly, *"Devageet, put the gas on for me."*

I foresaw that this would be another difficulty for the specialist to handle. I told him that Osho usually had nitrous oxide analgesia for all his dental procedures, and he was asking for it now.

The specialist said peevishly, "No, he can't have

that. It will mask his pain response."

Realizing that this was a potent moment of disagreement, I said carefully, "I realize that while this may be unusual in the United States, in England, it is routine. For Osho there are good, solid clinical reasons to use this method. The most important is that it will prevent Osho from having an asthma attack. Without it, even the smell of your aftershave might provoke status asthmaticus." He was visibly taken aback.

I went on, "And, you need not worry about the pain response being masked. You will find that even with this light analgesia, Osho is easily able to respond accurately to whatever sensations your tests create. He is very, very sensitive, he will respond to all your tests easily. But most of all, the nitrous will help to prevent an avoidable serious clinical emergency in this small room. As you can see there is very little space to move around. If Osho collapsed we would be in real trouble to treat him."

My point was well made. If Osho needed emergency medical treatment we would have to move everybody out to bring in a stretcher. The little room was full of large people.

Osho asked what was the trouble. I briefly explained the hitch.

Osho then directly addressed the specialist, *"It is okay. You need not worry. My body will be able to give you the accurate response to your tests. This gas is only to relax my body and my chest. Without it I may have an attack."*

I repeated Osho's words.

The specialist said, "Look, all this is very different from the way I usually work." He took a deep breath, before adding, "And are you sure we can elicit the pain response?"

I reassured him, saying, "Osho will be able to easily answer your questions, but he will not move his body in response to any pain that he might feel. He feels everything but he does not react to what he feels. I will interpret everything and I am sure that your tests will give you the diagnostic results."

Without waiting for his reply, I moved to the gas machine and turned the dials. Ashu placed the nose mask carefully. I reclined the dental chair to the full supine position, murmuring that in this position, there would be less possibility of a drop in Osho's blood pressure.

The room became completely silent except for the sounds from the respirator bag and the gentle hiss of gases. The silence appeared to increase the discomfort of the specialist. The whole situation was far beyond the "normal" and the "expected".

His nurse, meanwhile, had returned and presented the vitality tester to her boss. Behind her surgical mask, I could see she was smiling warmly at Osho.

As the silence deepened the specialist became even more disturbed. "Is he always as relaxed and quiet as this?" he asked. I guessed he thought Osho's extreme

The Fearful Specialist

stillness mean that he was in a state of anaesthetic sleep. "Look, I don't think this is going to work. Take that thing off."

I tried to get him to understand: "Even when Osho is simply sitting still he is a quiet and motionless as this. This deep relaxed state is normal for him. It is not the gas." But the specialist's emotional agitation prevented him from getting the point. The only people he would have seen in such a deeply relaxed state would have been under general anaesthesia.

"No. Take it off!" he barked.

I asked Ashu to remove the nose mask. Osho stayed silent and unmoving, with his eyes closed. The silence in the tiny dental room deepened, and to our amazement big tears began to roll down Osho's cheeks!

I looked at Ashu in disbelief. Vivek and Devaraj were staring, shocked.

The specialist's dental nurse took Osho's hand and murmured compassionately, "Oh my, oh my. Is it so, so painful? Oh, my poor dear." She looked appealingly towards her chief who stood as if transfixed. He gruffly indicated that it would be okay for me to resume the dental analgesia.

Ashu dried Osho's tears carefully before placing the mask back on his nose. The visiting nurse meantime was still holding Osho's left hand tenderly, her eyes soft and motherly.

I wondered what would happen next.

The specialist placed the vitality tester again on one of Osho's teeth, noting with satisfaction that the red light glowed, but as he watched, it faded to a glimmer, and then vanished. He frowned in perplexity. This was beyond anything he could explain. He neither knew what to say or how to react. He was stunned.

He withdrew the device, tapped it on his palm, muttering that it had never behaved like this before. The red light reappeared briefly before again dying.

He then became furious. "Are you sure you changed these batteries? Are these new batteries?" he barked at his unfortunate assistant. "And what about the bulb? It's probably the bulb!"

"Excuse me," I said, interrupting him, "it's not that unusual. Around Osho electrical appliances often behave strangely …"

My words, instead of appeasing him, seemed only to increase his discomfiture. "No, no, it's either the batteries or the bulb. She must have put in batteries from a dud batch."

His dental assistant shook her head nervously, not wanting to disagree with her boss, but not wanting him to blame her either. "No, doctor, these were new batteries straight from a new packet."

Meanwhile Osho was silent and still as the drama surged around him.

Devaraj and Vivek joined in the efforts to calm the specialist. "Oh it's nothing to worry about," said Vivek

The Fearful Specialist

lightly, as if the paranormal was commonplace for her. "His TV often goes wrong, stops, and when we get the electronics experts, they can find nothing wrong. They check everything; everything works while they're testing it, then the moment Osho enters the room the TV won't work anymore. It's not your nurse's fault. The batteries are probably not dud, but Osho's electricity is more powerful, or something."

Devaraj offered more consolatory words, "Yes, it's nothing to be concerned about. In fact it's perfectly normal around Osho." He laughed briefly, "I will find some more batteries and put them in, but don't worry if the machine packs up. It's routine around Osho." He laughed again, hoping to defuse the situation.

It was plain that the specialist found the situation more than he could handle. Anutosh then stepped in, adding helpfully, "Why not try percussion again now that Osho is receiving analgesia?"

The specialist brusquely handed the vitality tester back to his nurse, who handed it to Devaraj. He automatically flicked the switch: the red light glowed! The specialist saw it and it only added to his confusion. He resumed his percussion of the teeth with considerable force.

After each wallop, I asked Osho, "Did that cause pain?"

He merely grunted. But when the lower left first molar was struck, he said quietly, *"Geet, this tooth is the one. Every tooth he hits is painful but when he hits this one the pain is terrible."*

Anxious to halt the procedure, I told the specialist that he had successfully located the painful tooth. He looked relieved, and proceeded to probe for cavities, calling for recent x-rays. No obvious cause for the pain was visible. He then took a small penlight and shone it on the tooth. Half the tooth glowed brightly; the remaining half was dull grey.

"Here it is! This is the cause of the pain," he announced in triumph. "You see, it's a vertical hairline fracture!" He happily showed the illuminated tooth, half-grey and half-white, to Anutosh and myself. Devaraj and Vivek came too, muttering appreciatively on seeing the clearly demarcated tooth. The specialist's tension visibly melted in the warmth of approval and success.

He had saved the day. Meanwhile Osho was silent and still, apparently oblivious to things around him, but we knew better.

The specialist said, "Okay, now we've got it. The diagnosis is clear. This tooth, by the very nature of its fracture – look, the line goes straight through the root – can't be saved. A complicated root canal treatment with root hemi-section might have a small chance of success, but it's not likely. This tooth needs to be extracted. I can do it now, if you want me to."

I looked across at Devaraj. It was true, the tooth would need to be extracted, but this was not the man,

The Fearful Specialist

nor the time, to do it. His emotional state made him too heavy handed.

Devaraj, grasping the situation, stood up quickly and said, "Yes, that was a brilliant piece of diagnosis, doctor, perfect. Now, we will have to consider the surgical options carefully in the light of Osho's overall medical condition. We can discuss it more fully upstairs over a cup of tea, but because of his diabetes, it will probably be better to put him on a course of antibiotic therapy to cover any eventuality of post-operative infection, maybe even a course of steroids. Perhaps you and I could discuss the medical problems further in the support trailer. We can safely leave Osho to the dentists while we talk over the surgical risks and clinical options," he said, gently taking the specialist's arm and leading him from the dental cabin. His nurse, who had been holding Osho's left hand throughout, reluctantly let it go before dutifully following her chief.

I breathed a huge sigh of relief, before saying, "The dental treatment is over for today, Osho. I'll turn on the oxygen."

He nodded almost imperceptibly, before saying, *"Two minutes for me, Geet."*

In the ensuing deeply familiar, throbbing silence, Ashu, Vivek, Anutosh and I meditated by his side, until I heard his soft voice say, *"Geet, enough for today."*

Chapter II
"You can kill me but do not harm my moustache ..."

From 1987 onwards, during his dental sessions, there were many times when Osho would speak while I was using the dental drill on his teeth. As Osho's personal dentist, I had the finest instruments available, and I loved to use them to the best of my ability. Their purposeful design was a delight. Their edges were sharp, their effect was precise, and the outcome of a clinical session could be predicted within the limits of one's own expertise – except with Osho.

Dentistry is an artisan surgical science where great attention to detail is important for the best clinical and aesthetic outcome. The methods of dental restoration and surgery are many and varied and the numerous instruments express a history of mechanical ingenuity manifested in stainless steel for the arcane purposes of attaining clinical dental excellence that nobody except the professionals know or care about.

Time and again, Osho would deliberately shatter the field of concentration needed in order to complete his dental work painlessly and skillfully. I was his dentist and his disciple, and he, as my spiritual master, engaged in bizarre strategies to sabotage the mental concentration required for dental work as he laboured to liberate the disciple into higher realms of consciousness.

In addition to normal dental operating hazards, Osho's mouth was framed in exuberant, abundantly sprouting hair. His beard was a vital living thing, it was continuously growing, seemingly becoming thicker and longer by the day. At the times of his last appointments, his beard reached below his waist, a vast waterfall of silvery strands, each one of which seemed to be stubbornly opposed to the practice of dentistry.

The actual guardian of Osho's oral cavity was his moustache. Thick, wide, deep and full, it maintained a dental vigilance that forced me to respect its intention while simultaneously attempting to circumvent its undoubted efforts to keep me out. I knew Osho's moustache had nothing personal against me; after all, it had its job to do, but I was clearly regarded as an intruder, a persona non grata, an invader, a disciple deigning to get at the teeth of the master. Osho was amused by the whole dental drama on several levels, especially, I suspect, by my puny attempts to domesticate his wild and willful moustache.

The first time Osho spontaneously started to speak during a dental session I was taken completely by surprise. His mouth, while he remained silent, was usually utterly still, a perfect operating area except that it was small, and crowded with instruments and fingers. But as long as his cheeks and tongue were immobile I could happily manage the dental variables and do my work well. On this occasion, without warning, he started to speak! His tongue moved, instantly flicking saliva-soaked cottonwool rolls into the path of the high-speed drill. The sodden rolls, caught in the diamond tip, continued to rotate at 400,000 revolutions per minute, spraying his new dental nurse, Nityamo, his secretary, Anando, who sat at his right elbow, and me copiously with saliva.

The blur of the rapidly revolving cotton roll was accompanied by a distinct buzzing sound, as if a very large bumblebee was trapped inside his mouth, the cavity of which acted as a resonator. Not only that, the cotton roll was beating the underside of Osho's tongue as it rotated madly. I noticed bluish bruises appearing almost instantly on his delicate tissues.

To say I was shocked would be to minimise the extreme effect his sudden, unexpected speaking had on my nervous system, My whole physiology stopped in its tracks in that unforgettable moment. My blood ran icy cold. It seemed to congeal in my veins. My heart was thumping and my hands were trembling.

Utter surprise and sheer disbelief robbed me of any quick reactions. I sat on my operator's stool while being sprayed for a number of seconds before I realized what was happening. My operating glasses had become like a car's windscreen caught in a sudden heavy downpour. Through the blur, as my nervous system began to function again, I recognized the danger and took my foot from the switch governing the drill.

Gingerly, I took the slim, steel cylinder of a drill from Osho's mouth. I attempted to remove the mangled cotton roll. He continued to speak as he lay supine, his eyes closed. His words were a little slurred by the effect of local anaesthesia on his tongue, but slow and clear as always, and his voice was soft and low. Apparently, for him, nothing was amiss, although he was clearly aware of the mayhem he had created. For my dentally-focussed psyche, everything was a mess.

I motioned to Nityamo to change the drill while she was quietly handing tissues to Anando as we sat listening to him. He was speaking to Anando. She was as astonished as me. Osho had often spoken to her before, or following, the dental operation, but never in the middle of it. She had been sitting with her eyes closed, meditating, when in an instant she heard his voice and had simultaneously been sprayed with saliva from a rapidly revolving cotton wool roll that made a noise like a buzzsaw. His words, however, emerged unscathed through the spray. After a few moments, he stopped speaking and opened his mouth for the dental action to resume, as if nothing had happened.

I was nervous, unsure of what to do or say. I needed to change the dental drill and substitute the cotton-clogged handpiece for a new one. I had three spare handpieces, but they were not designed for such treatment. It was the equivalent of throwing a forward moving car into reverse. The miniature ball bearings inside the handpiece could easily be shattered by such a manoeuvre.

"Osho," I said slowly. My voice was trembling from the shock. "Do you think you could give me a sign that you want to speak before you actually move your tongue? I need a little warning in order to move all the dental stuff out of the way and prevent any harm to you, and the drill …"

My words sank without trace into the silence of his presence. Osho's silence was qualitatively and perceptibly different from simple quietness. It was thick and tangible. Any words that emerged did so as if they were surprised at having successfully made the journey.

Quietly, he said, *"If you want me to stop speaking, Devageet, I will stop speaking forever."* I was stunned. "Oh no!" I said impulsively. The possibility that I would never hear his voice again was terrible. Osho's speaking was a highlight in my life even before meeting him. Many years previously, before I had journeyed to India, I had written to the ashram in Pune for some of his discourses on audiotape. His voice on tape had been my first physical connection with him. I deeply valued hearing Osho speak, but this was different; it was incredibly dangerous, the drill could cut through steel. His tongue was numb and by speaking he could easily have put it in the path of the drill. This was about dentistry, or was it?

And stopping speaking forever? No more discourses? Hundreds of thousands of people no longer able to hear his voice, receive his wisdom? The very thought was too horrible to contemplate.

"Oh no, Osho, I love to hear you speak" I said. "But suddenly speaking while this high-speed drill is in your mouth is extremely dangerous. It could slip and easily cut your tongue or cheeks. If you could give me a small sign I could stop immediately. It would make it safer and easier for you to speak."

He chuckled slightly, his shoulders joining in the merriment. Osho had a wonderful throaty chuckle.

Devageet, you do not understand. I speak when I need to speak. I do not choose. Existence is speaking through me. 'Now' is always my time. I speak spontaneously. Nothing on earth, or beyond this earth, can stop me speaking. Even when I am no longer in the body I will continue to speak. It is only speaking to my people that keeps me alive in this body. I have been speaking continuously for my whole life. It is my only work, and you want to stop it.

I understood. I wanted him to speak. I wanted him never to stop. But if he spoke while I was drilling I did not know if I could keep him safe and the potential for disaster was too awful to contemplate.

Thus it was on the day of the moustache. On this occasion I wanted to do what is popularly known as a "scale and polish." Nothing dangerous, except that the slow-speed dental drill equipped with a tiny bristle brush to clean his front teeth could easily get caught up in his massive moustache that hung precipitously over his top lip. Working on his front teeth I would have to hold his lip, with its anarchistic moustache, clear of the drill. Provided he didn't speak it would be relatively easy to keep his moustache safe. If he spoke, then his moustache would instantly be wound up in the revolving brush. I explained this to Osho.

"Devageet, you can kill my body but do not harm my moustache," he said gently but with an emphasis that was unmissable.

He did not mention speaking, or not, but I certainly heard how he felt about his moustache.

I started slowly, very alert and careful. Osho was still and silent. The silence in the room deepened as all the people present entered into their meditation.

Suddenly he spoke!

Instantly the brush caught the overhanging hair of his moustache, tangling it massively into the drill head. I swiftly removed my foot from the foot pedal switch, and loosened my grip on the drill in an effort to minimise the amount of moustache that was being plucked out as the drill ground to a halt. The drill dangled forlornly on its metal overhead supporting arm. It was still attached to his moustache.

I was again shocked. I had been warned but could not prevent this hairy disaster.

Nityamo, Osho's dental nurse, looked unblinkingly at the mass of moustache entangled in the drill head.

Slowly, large full tears emerged from beneath her round spectacles, briefly visible before dissolving into widening grey damp patches in her absorbent surgical facemask.

Carefully I examined the extent of the tangle to see if it would be possible to retrieve and save any of the mass of hairs wound around the tiny brush and up into the drill head. Removing the brush I painstakingly unwound each hair of the beloved moustache, unaware of my own tears until my own mask became sodden. With tweezers, one by one, I managed to extract most of the hairs. I then took the drillhead apart in an attempt to salvage the few remaining strands wound into the gears and mashed into the ball bearings.

As I worked I saw there was grease and oil staining Osho's lip and his now-ragged moustache. Nityamo, working painstakingly slowly, gently cleaned his lip and moustache with a cotton bud, her slim fingers stroking his moustache apologetically back into place. But there were four long hairs that were irretrievably mangled into the miniature machinery.

During the whole episode Osho had said nothing. He had stopped speaking instantly as soon as the accident occurred.

I was feeling wretched as I said, "Osho, I have managed to free most of your moustache but there are four hairs that I cannot save. I am sorry. I will have to cut them." My voice echoed my sadness.

Osho said nothing. The silence was immense.

I held the four moustache hairs with forceps while Nityamo cut them close to their roots. These four faithful hairs had been terminated by my dental drill. It was a bereavement. I loved his magnificent moustache even though it made my work hazardous. I knew I could not have done anything differently but the recognition did not affect my feelings of sadness or diminish my sense of responsibility.

I spoke. "Osho, I will have to continue the tooth cleaning on another day. I am too shaky now. I am sorry."

He remained utterly silent.

A few moments I added quietly into his ear, "The dentistry is finished for today."

Osho stayed still. We all sat quiet, with our eyes closed, waiting for him to signal that he was ready for the dental chair to be returned to the upright position. The room, with its five disciples sitting around their master, was in deep silence.

After a few moments he motioned slightly with his head. I pressed the switch and the chair hummed back into the vertical position. Vivek placed his sandals beside his feet for him to slip them on. She then stood. He rose slowly and gracefully, turned to us, namasted each of us in turn, then walked out, taking Vivek's hand as he left the dental room.

Nityamo kept those terminated moustache hairs in safekeeping.

Chapter 12
Closure Osho Style

At the beginning of our master-dental-disciple relationship, Osho was the model dental patient. During each session he would sit perfectly still and silent, uncannily so. Even his eyeballs under his closed lids never moved, nor his tongue. He neither swallowed nor moved a muscle. It felt to me as if his consciousness left his body and travelled somewhere else, knowing and trusting that Ashu and I would take good care of it.

There were several unusual features about Osho's dental tissues. Most people receiving a dental injection show an involuntary rejection response. Tiny muscles in their mucous membranes automatically contract away from the point of the long needle. But Osho's membranes showed no aversion reaction.

Most adult teeth show a reduction in the size of the dental nerves as they become worn with age. However, despite heavy attrition, due to his youthful experiments with diet and food, when he had restricted his diet to grains and beans, cooked and uncooked, Osho's teeth showed remarkably large and vital nerves. They were comparable to those of a young child, while the outer enamel and dentine showed the excessive wear and tear of an old adult. It was a dental paradox. Working on his teeth I could see the pink nerve tissue shining through the translucent biting surface. I guessed that would make his teeth unusually sensitive to pain, but he never showed it.

At Rancho Rajneesh, Osho spoke after each dental session was completed. I would say to him, "Osho, the dental work is finished now."

Usually he waited a moment before saying quietly, *"Okay Geet, now is my time. Now I begin my work on you. Remember, I may be in the dental chair but you are on my operating table."*

In February 1982, Osho finished dictating from the dental chair the notes that would later form three books: "Notes Of A Madman", "Books I Have Loved" and "Glimpses Of A Golden Childhood". There was a gap of several months before he called for his next series of dental sessions. During those sessions he was still and silent during the dental work, although occasionally he spoke at length before or afterwards.

In 1987, he returned to the ashram in Pune. The old dental room in Lao Tzu House was refurbished and newly equipped. I travelled to London, to the same dental showroom as before, and ordered the latest models of exactly the same dental machinery as I had purchased in 1980.

Nityamo was now Osho's personal dental nurse. Osho was forced to travel from country to country due to American government harassment preventing him from settling in a new country and creating a new commune for his work to continue. At the outset of what Osho called his "world tour," Ashu, his dental nurse, had been among Osho's accompanying household staff. Along the way, she had fallen in love with a handsome Russian while Osho briefly sojourned in Nepal on his world tour. Nityamo became Osho's dental nurse and Ashu was living a life of chaotic domestic bliss in Kathmandu.

Nityamo and I had been lovers since 1982. Osho's deportation from America, and the subsequent breakup of Rajneeshpuram, had created upheaval in our lives. Our romance and attempts to remain in loving harmony had been severely battered and dented by our many adventures. We continued to love each other, but the stresses were becoming too obvious to avoid.

Since arriving back in Pune, Nitty and I began to argue over small things. We had always had our differences, but now the healing time for our lovers' tiffs stretched on for days. One unhealed tiff joined seamlessly to the next. We were both aware of our relationship troubles, but we could not help ourselves. One night, following a spat because I wanted to keep the light on so I could read, and she wanted it off so she could sleep, I remember complaining, "Nitty, what kind of freedom is this if I cannot even read in bed?"

Unbeknownst to me, she wrote a letter to Osho asking for guidance on how to handle our crumbling love affair.

It was midnight three weeks later: Nitty and I were sitting together on the roof of Lao Tzu House before going to bed. It was a wide, shining, white-tiled terrace overhung with great trees and frangipani blossoms, idyllic under the moonlight. We had long since shelved our hurts in favour of the joys of being together.

I could see Vivek approaching in the bright moonlight. She came and sat close to Nitty and without preamble said, "Osho got your letter, Nitty. He has not forgotten to reply. For these last few weeks he has been watching you both."

Startled, I looked at Nitty. She was looking wide-eyed at Vivek, stunned. This was the first I had known of her letter to Osho. Vivek, a veteran of several relationship campaigns, appeared cool, aloof and untouched.

She went on, "Osho has given me a message for both of you. He says that it would be best if you split up. You can still be friends but it would be best if you live apart. There is no rush for you to decide, but when you do, he told me to create new living arrangements for you both. Devageet can move in and share a room with Devaraj. Nitty, you can share your room with Nirupa. It can be done easily and quickly, in a way that not many people will notice and gossip."

Because of the speed and unexpectedness of events, I was feeling a confused mixture of astonishment, shock and delight. Osho's suggestions offered the perfect solution to our imperfect situation. I glanced at Nitty. She looked pale and shaky, or maybe it was the moonlight.

Vivek added, "Should you both decide to split up

within the next twenty-four hours it would be even better. You can let me know tomorrow, at breakfast time." And without a backward glance she walked away into the moonshadows of the night.

Sitting in the ensuing silence I suddenly remembered that Vivek was at the tail end of her own relationship too. And Devaraj? How could I move in with him? Wasn't he living with Maneesha? Perhaps they too were splitting up. "My God," I thought, "it looks as though a major relationship reshuffle is happening."

On the roof terrace where we had our room Nitty and I sat in outer silence and inner turmoil for some minutes. I could feel unspoken thoughts and feelings jostling together in the space between us. Tentatively we slowly opened our hearts to each other. Through the curtain of our hesitant words and fears of being apart we began to recognise the gift Osho was offering. We decided to make the jump.

Following our moonlit discussion, strangely, we became more passionate and loving than we had been for many months. We hadn't split up yet, but I was already missing her.

Early the next day, Nitty and I made our way down the wrought iron spiral staircase that led from the roof terrace to the ground floor of Lao Tzu House. We almost bumped into Vivek as she was returning Osho's breakfast dishes to the kitchen. We told her of our decision and she appeared very happy that we had been able to decide so quickly. She said that she would tell Osho and then let us know about our new living arrangements.

Later the same day Vivek delivered another message: Nitty and I were to come to a meeting involving some other couples who were also living in Lao Tzu House.

The meeting took place in Hasya's large room. Hasya, a sophisticated, cool, capable Hollywood lady, had been Osho's international secretary since Sheela's departure. It was a difficult role during Osho's world tour. In her room were five other couples, including Vivek's partner, Rafia. It seemed that there was a small epidemic of breaking relationships.

The message from Osho was read out by Vivek. It started by reminding us that we were all mature, meditative people, and long-time sannyasins, and that we had all been with him long enough to understand the deeper implications of the message that we were about to receive. He told us that the relationship we were now ending was to be our last. We were to separate from our current lovers without clinging, and, though we could still be friends, we should allow the relationship to end in an atmosphere of loving gratitude. We should let each other know how much we had valued and enjoyed our time together; and recognizing that the love between us had changed and cooled, it was time for the relationship to end. Although we could have lovers in the future, we would not have relationships.

Osho's message went on, saying that friendship is a

higher quality than relationship, and friendliness was an even higher quality. In our maturity, Osho reassured us we would find the truth of his words for ourselves.

The message continued: If, after the separation, we happened to see our old lover with a new friend, we were not to be jealous. We should simply remain alert, meditative and watchful for our old conditioned mind's habitual reaction to slip into jealousy and blame.

He told us that we had been chosen to be his first sannyasins to live his vision for mature men and women. We had been chosen because he could see that we were now able to live together as individuals, free from any relationship, living in a new, conscious way – relating, but not in relationship.

He affirmed that the old style of relationship was over, and we should be happy at the news. The old way of relating had brought us much misery along with its few pleasures. We should let it go, along with the suffering, the jealousy and the possessiveness that had been part of what we had each been living in the name of love up till this time of change.

Osho said that he knew that we could all do it, and that it would be easy for us. He was happy to see that the time was right for us to make this new jump, that so many of us had reached the same point at the same time. And, he said, sannyasins on the outside of Lao Tzu House would see and take example from us. He told us that he had been waiting for this time, the time when his people were ready to relate in a new way, as mature men and women. He was happy that the time had finally arrived, and we should be too.

Vivek summarized his vision and told us:

"The world is ready for the New Man, and the old style of relationship has to be dropped along with the old conditioning. The New Man is able to relate easily and freely with others, valuing friendliness as a higher value than the old style of possessive, clinging relationship, even higher than friendship: friendship is still a 'ship,' it can sink. Mature people can be loving without being possessive; they can live together in freedom without jealousy."

I looked around; the mood of the others appeared to match my own, a mixture of stunned amazement, enthusiasm and downright fear. Looking inside I could feel that I was ready for the new experiment, but I looked in vain for the confidence in myself that Osho's message had implied.

Later that day Vivek told me that my new room space in Devaraj's room, directly above Osho's ground floor bedroom, was available. It had a large, open balcony, level with the tops of the great trees in Osho's garden.

Standing on the balcony, I was at the same height as the branches, listening to the wind among the leaves, and the birds chattering. I was entranced. On the balcony

I felt wonderfully free, and I decided to move my bed and desk there, to make it my new living space. The only change needed was to cover the whole balcony area with mosquito netting and to equip it with monsoon storm blinds.

Nitty was a little tearful when she came to see my new space, but having two rooms gave more space for our new expanded intimacy. I felt very happy. I still loved Nitty but was relieved to be no longer tied together by the unspoken contracts of domestication that had been strangling our individual freedom … and I could read in bed without feeling guilty.

On learning of my first date with a new friend, Nitty was deeply upset. Afterwards she and I sat together and tried to be mature, without much success. When she found a new friend, I was frantic. I realized that my own concept of freedom was severely limited: freedom was fine as long as it was mine.

Over the next months, Nitty and I both moved deeper into the new maturity that Osho's gift had opened for us, but the old habits of immaturity were powerfully present much of the time, grinning spectres mocking my attempts to live in new way.

At the commencement of one dental session during this emotionally turbulent time, as Osho was lying silent and still in his dental chair, he suddenly said quietly, *"Devageet, I can hear your heart sobbing."*

Yet again I was shocked by Osho's clarity. It was

true. The previous evening Nitty had told me that she had fallen in love. My heart felt as though it was breaking. At Osho's words I realized that he must be aware of all the emotional crosscurrents we each brought into his presence. Ashamed, I tried to put aside my emotions and turn to the dental work in hand.

Osho was training me, working on me, preparing me, to be focused and alert despite any personal emotional upheavals. He was my master and I was his dentist and his disciple, and my private emotional dramas had no place between us. They were a distraction. The only way for me to keep my emotions out of the sacred space between Osho and myself was to be increasingly aware of my inner world and not be automatically driven by each storm. His words became my mirror.

During a dental session soon afterwards, while drilling away an old filling, as I was intently working at the back of his mouth, fully concentrating on protecting his moustache, tongue and cheeks, he suddenly closed his mouth! The high speed air-turbine drill was still going full speed as he firmly brought his teeth together!

My mind stopped in sheer astonished disbelief. It took me milliseconds for the situation to register. The psychological impact of his utterly unexpected and profoundly dangerous move was colossal.

In sheer horror I saw his lips and teeth together as I still held the drill. It was held firmly between his teeth. I let it go, gazing in disbelief as it protruded from his mouth, emerging through the hair of his moustache like a metallic cigar.

He remained still and utterly silent. The drill was forced deep through his tooth into his jaw.

Slowly my mind took stock of the situation, disbelieving, yet observing. I tried not to think of the consequences of Osho's mouth closure. The diamond-tipped drill could have easily sliced through the soft tissues beneath his tongue, and there were arteries and nerves, glands and .... I shuddered at the thought. I knew the drill might have sliced in the other direction, into the soft tissues of his cheek. I had seen such accidents during my hospital training. They had required plastic surgery to heal the wounds. I shuddered in horror again. At the very least, the drill may have been driven vertically into the hard tissue of the tooth, penetrating into the root tissues and maybe the bone of attachment itself.

Every possibility, as it offered itself on the screen of my mind, was awful, differing only in magnitude. While these thoughts surfaced I was watching to see from where the blood would emerge. I was afraid to open his mouth to see the extent of the damage. I was in shock.

The silence in the dental room was intense. As I sat waiting for the next move in this bizarre dental drama, I could feel myself getting angry. It was bad enough that this emergency situation had been created, but now I needed to take action to limit the effects.

Osho remained silent, his eyes closed, with the drill

poking from between his lips. On some level it was comical to see. In reality, I was horrified.

I said angrily, "Osho, closing your mouth like that on a moving drill is incredibly dangerous. You may have badly damaged your tongue, your teeth, your lips and cheeks. I'm too freaked out to even look. Why did you close your mouth like that?"

There was no response from Osho, only a deepening silence in the room. Everybody was in shock. We were in a dental nightmare.

Again I tried, "If you wanted me to stop, why didn't you give me a sign, an indication? But to clamp your teeth together like that is so dangerous, I can't even believe it has happened. I need to look inside your mouth and see what has been damaged."

My words disappeared like vapor into the sky, seeming to have neither relevance nor meaning in the silence of that strange situation. The situation was as it was.

Bizarre and fearful though it appeared to my shocked mind, the silence was the same. Osho was the same. The is-ness of the moment was untouchable, intangible and unknowable. Osho's mouth closure had apparently stopped time and mind. My mind and its words were like a dog helplessly yapping at a stopped car.

My mind unfroze in layers. After my first angry reaction I was left uncertain how to proceed. I spoke to my silent, utterly relaxed patient, from whose mouth my dental drill poked out like a finger indicating something beyond my grasp. "Osho, I don't know why you suddenly closed your mouth on the drill but there is every possibility of severe damage inside it. I need to look in your mouth to see what I need to do next."

My words disappeared into the lake of his silence without leaving even a ripple.

I sat on my dental stool utterly confused. As I leaned forward to say something else Osho slowly began to open his mouth. I took hold of the drill in order to remove it. And he closed his jaws again.

I asked in sheer frustration, "Would you like me to take the drill from your mouth?" Again the words disappeared as if they had been addressed wrongly, a message delivered to an empty house, a dog barking at the moon.

I sat quietly, watching him carefully, aware of the turmoil inside me, helpless and unknowing, and that made it worse. I felt somewhere that my reaction was inappropriate, that I had failed to respond to some unknown challenge. I was missing something, but I had no eyes to see, no ears to hear. I was vaguely aware that Osho was pointing something out to me, and all I could see was my own mind, its fears for his safety, and my state-of-the-art dental drill framed by a magnificent moustache.

As I watched and agonized, he opened his mouth slowly once more. I reached tentatively for the now-drooping drill. Holding it, I could see and feel it had been driven deeply, vertically, into the molar I had been working on. Before I could extricate the drill, or look inside his mouth, he closed it again, jamming the drill into his tooth once again.

I took several deep breaths. "At least he isn't feeling any pain," I thought. "The local anaesthetic is deep enough to prevent him from feeling much."

He again opened his mouth a little, and again, as I took hold of the drill, he closed it. It was a bizarre game for which I did not know the rules. I could only stand on the sidelines and watch.

He half opened his mouth five times. Each time I tried to remove the drill he closed his mouth on it. If it weren't so dangerous it would have been funny. Somewhere I knew that for him it was funny. I imagined he was chuckling, waiting for me to join him and have a good belly laugh. For this remarkable man, in some inexplicable way, there was no danger, so why not sit back and enjoy the game.

Finally, I took hold of the drill as he opened his mouth yet again, alert in case he closed his teeth together once more. But he kept it open long enough for me to carefully lift the bloody drill from the tooth and look around inside his mouth. I was relieved to notice that there was no soft tissue damage. All I could assess in those brief moments was a deep vertical hole through the crown of his molar and apparently deep into the root structures and his jaw.

He gave me enough time and space to irrigate his tooth with sterile water, to dry it with sterile paper points and place an antibiotic dressing into the wound. By this time I was trembling so much that I could only manage to take an exploratory x-ray, and say, "Osho, I will have to continue tomorrow. I will look at the x-ray to see the damage, and tomorrow I can tell you what needs to be done. But for today, I'm finished."

As my words ended, the silence returned. We sat beside our master as if nothing had happened. My turbulent emotions became calm, and somewhere in my head I could hear an agonized mind searching helplessly for answers to this astonishing dental drama.

There were none.

After a time, Osho motioned with a slight movement of his head that the session was over. I pressed the button and the chair returned to the upright position. As always, he sat quietly as Vivek placed his feet in his sandals. Then, standing up Osho namasted us all in turn, as always. He left the dental room, gracefully, softly and silently, as always.

I quickly asked Nitty if she had seen anything that I had missed. Perhaps she had noticed why he had closed his mouth on the drill. She was too emotional to answer. She could only shake her head. I noticed that her surgical mask was wet with tears.

I waited for Vivek, knowing that soon she would

pass the dental room on her way to the kitchen to get Osho a drink. As she approached, I spoke to her, but she brushed me aside. She was doing her work, and had no time for any interruptions. As she bustled about in the kitchen, I asked if she would enquire of Osho why he had closed his mouth on the drill. I needed to know if I was responsible for his strange behavior. She nodded in assent, muttering only that she would ask him if a suitable situation present itself. I was left with myself, with my self-doubts, my fears, and a vast unknowing.

At the next day's dental session, having assessed the situation with the damaged molar, I told Osho that we would have to do a root canal, and with a good deal of luck, I might be able to repair the hole through the side of the root of his tooth. As I was speaking of his dental damage, I had the distinct feeling he was looking into my head and seeing the extent of my mental damage.

Osho never referred to this incident. In fact, he continued to do unexpected and potentially dangerous acts while I was working on his teeth. There was never any explanation.

Chapter 13
Osho's Last Dental Drama: Act I
The Ear, The Tooth, and Beyond

Osho was having another bout of severe pain in his ears. His medical team arranged to consult with Dr. Jog, the Pune ear-nose-throat specialist. The consultations were usually held in Osho's new dental room because the dental chair and the surgical lighting made Dr. Jog's work easier, and the chair was comfortable for Osho. I was on hand mainly to operate the chair.

Osho had suffered from intermittent bouts of severe ear pain since being deported from America. Their intensity and duration was increasing. On this occasion, Dr. Jog diagnosed a plug of wax in Osho's left ear as the probable cause. He softened the wax with emulsifying drops, and twenty-four hours later, deftly removed the plug from his motionless patient.

When the removal was finished, Osho asked Dr. Jog to look in his other ear to see what might be causing the pain there. After looking, Dr. Jog said there was a small amount of wax there too and that he would place drops of oil to soften it and then return tomorrow to excavate it. Osho nodded, before saying, *"My time is now Dr. Jog. You can remove it now."*

Dr. Jog was surprised and a little discomfited. I have

noticed that doctors become uneasy when their patients have a mind of their own. In this case, Osho was exhibiting a no-mind of his own, and the discomfiture was even more. Dr. Jog told Osho the procedure might prove very painful without prior softening of the wax. Osho simply nodded and asked him to go ahead and not to worry about the pain. *"The pain is my responsibility. My time is always now."*

Looking nervously mystified at these enigmatic statements, Dr. Jog began to probe the delicate tissue. Osho sat unmoving. Glancing anxiously at his patient from time to time, Dr. Jog completed excavating the wax from the surface of the eardrum and the inner walls of the ear. He was sweating profusely. Osho was cool and relaxed.

When the procedure was complete, Osho smiled before nodding gently to indicate I could bring the chair back to the vertical. Slowly and gracefully as ever, he slid his feet into the sandals placed in readiness by his caretaker ,Shunyo.

Later that day I was called for a dental session. At the commencement, Osho told me that his right ear was deeply painful and asked whether the pain could be coming from a tooth. I nodded, adding that I would need to examine the area and take a couple of x-rays to assess the situation, but that the most probable cause for the pain might be the operation performed earlier in the day by Dr. Jog, and it might be best to wait for twenty-four hours to see if the pain decreased.

The next day Osho again called for a session that included Dr. Jog and me. It was also attended by Devaraj, Nityamo, Shunyo and Anando, as was usual for dental sessions in those days.

Dr. Jog examined both ears and could find no obvious cause for the pain. Osho asked me if my dental x-ray examination had shown a likely dental cause. I explained that there was nothing conclusive but the right lower wisdom tooth looked heavily worn with some periodontal involvement. "It's not in great shape but it will last for some time. I doubt whether it is the cause of your ear pain, but it is possible."

Osho asked how we could rule out a dental cause for his ear pain. It was a difficult question with no definite answer. I said, "Well, if the tooth is the cause, then removing the tooth would probably get rid of the pain. But there's no way for me to be certain that the pain is caused by the tooth. We might remove the tooth and still be left with the pain."

Osho listened and then said, *"Take the tooth out now. My time is always now."*

I looked across at Devaraj. I did not relish extracting a tooth for Osho, especially a lower wisdom tooth. I had extracted one of his molars once before, with great effect, but I didn't like doing surgery on Osho. Putting needles into him and drilling his teeth was bad enough, but extracting a wisdom tooth was not my idea of fun with

The Ear, The Tooth, and Beyond

anybody, especially not with my spiritual Master. I didn't like doing any dental procedure on him that might create pain. But, after all, I was his dentist.

Devaraj pursed his lips, shrugging slightly, as if to signify, "Osho has said what he wants."

Osho added that he would leave the surgery briefly to relieve the pressure on his bladder, and when he returned we could take the tooth out. I was grateful for the short intermission because Nityamo would need a little time to set up the surgery ready for the extraction.

Dr. Jog was also relieved. I could see from his pale face that watching a wisdom tooth being extracted was a long way down his list of desirable ways to spend an afternoon.

As Nityamo and I laid out the surgical instruments, I was apprehensive about Osho going straight from the surgery into Buddha Hall for the evening meditation meeting. I knew that, in all probability, he would dance energetically from the podium with his people in the huge audience.

Osho's dancing was a unique art form. He would stand during the evening meditation, facing the crowd of dancing, clapping, white-robed sannyasins, beating time with both hands, moving his arms and shoulders in what appeared to be the rhythm of the music.

But appearances with Osho hide a deeper reality. He would usually start slowly, slower than the music, and the musicians would slow down their music. He would speed up, and again the musicians would try to keep pace.

The loose sleeves on his magnificent robes would sway and flap madly as he took control of the beat, winding it up to a level where the musicians mostly lost all semblance of control, often dissolving into a frenzied wild dissonance, with only Nivedano, Osho's brilliant Brazilian drummer-percussionist, managing to stay in rhythm with the Master.

Each evening, as the musicians were swept into their evening device with the Master, the audience of hundreds of sannyasins would be ecstatically clapping, swaying and dancing as Osho's dancing brought the energy in Buddha Hall to a crescendo. As the energy peaked, Osho would signal with his hand, and Nivedano would give three mighty drumbeats, each followed by the audience loudly shouting 'OSHO!" Osho would then quietly and gracefully namaste his "ten thousand Buddhas," and take his seat in silence. His stillness and grace guided the joyous energy in Buddha Hall into a pin-drop silence as each person directed their energy inwards.

In those peak-energy-filled fifteen minutes of inner silence and soft outer music that followed the three drumbeats, our dancing hearts, filled with the wild joy of being with Osho, were open to feel the rush of bliss as existence itself filled the screen of our awareness. It was a daily, hilarious climax, a mind-dissolving mixture of laughter, dancing, joy and jubilation that heralded the beginning of each evening's meditation with the Master. This was the Master at work: Each night Osho created devices to enable his sannyasins to experience for themselves the blissful no-mind state that arises when an individual directly encounters the is-ness, the existential reality, of here-and-now.

During the preceding year, Osho had been meticulously orchestrating the evening meditation meeting. Earlier in the year he had requested us to wear simple, plain white robes for the evening meditation, and what had been known as "Osho's Discourse," he renamed as, "The Evening Meeting of The Osho White Robe Brotherhood."

For many months, he had been modifying and refining the sequence of the component parts of the evening meditation: fifteen minutes of music and celebration and dancing with the Master, followed by music and silent meditation in his silent presence, followed by his spoken discourse, concluding with a meditation guided by Osho himself.

The Evening Meeting of The Osho White Robe Brotherhood was carefully and systematically developed by Osho as an objective art form designed to enable participating individuals to personally experience the no-mind perception of one's own core-of-being: the essence of Osho's meditation.

Jokes were always an important aspect of every Osho discourse. He was perhaps the first enlightened master to use laughter for healing and transformation. It has since been found that laughter induces the production of endorphins, Nature's life-enhancing hormones. He used humour in many ways: to sharpen our intelligence, to open our eyes to any hidden prejudices hiding beneath the hilarity, to dislodge our most stubborn conditioning, and mostly to relax and open our hearts and minds to the simple joy of being alive. Osho considered seriousness a deadly disease, an ego-disease that can easily smother the flame in the heart of every true seeker by encouraging a holier-than-thou attitude.

Occasionally, to add to the general air of festive celebration and jokiness, Osho, ably assisted by Anando and Avirbhava, would host a parade of toy animals to jokingly remind us that many worldwide religious beliefs include ancient animal deities. These events were known as the "Museum of Ancient Gods."

During all my years with Osho, I had never seen him put such attention into the form and structure of any other meditation event as he did for The Evening Meeting of the White Robe Brotherhood. It was clearly of great significance. Occasionally, during an evening dental session that followed the Evening Meeting, he would ask, *"How was the meeting tonight, Geet?"* and listen carefully to my feedback. He would often ask the same question of Nityamo, and Shunyo told me he frequently asked her or Vivek that question as they accompanied him in the Rolls as he drove back from Buddha Hall to Lao Tzu

House.

Osho later instructed his sannyasins:

"All my people should attend each Evening Meeting of The White Robe Brotherhood, and my sannyasins around the world should all follow the same format. In this way, sannyasins will be creating a global energy field of meditation, because around the world, during the twenty-four hour day, it is always seven o'clock somewhere on earth. The evening meeting of the Osho White Robe Brotherhood is the most important time of any sannyasin's day."

It was only after he had left his body did I realize that during this preparatory period Osho had been creating an energy vehicle, a ritual, for his people to connect with him each night.

Dentally speaking, it was abundantly clear that Osho's exuberant dancing would not provide the ideal healing environment for his extraction socket. I knew that Osho never acted out of fear of any negative consequences. My own fears, however, knew no such limitation. I trusted that love, joy and meditation are more effective healers than simple caution, but I was apprehensive for his health.

The operation to remove his wisdom tooth was quick and easy. The extraction was clean and simple, and I placed three silk sutures to minimize any post-operative bleeding and reduce the likelihood of subsequent infection. I did everything I could, and afterwards could only step back to wait and see.

Following the short surgical operation, the dental team happily left the magnificent new dental room and we readied ourselves for the evening meditation. Less than an hour later, Osho was in full flood, his glorious celebrating energy setting the standard for us all in Buddha Hall. Seeing his vitality, his abandoned dancing and self-evident joy I could only marvel once again at this remarkable man. But I was worried about the three dental sutures.

Osho didn't call for a dental session during the next two days. My nervousness subsided into a sporadic twitch that only surfaced when I thought about his diminished healing capacity. Since leaving the United States his body had shown a dramatic reduction in its immune response. In addition, his physical resources were severely depleted, and he suffered chronic, intractable bone pain, and other puzzling, serious symptoms.

In 1987, during a morning discourse following yet another bout of mysterious debilitating illness, Osho informed his startled sannyasins that clinical pathological evidence, along with his physical signs and symptoms, suggested that his increasing debility and illness were due to having been poisoned by the American authorities, probably using thallium, while being held in United States jails after his illegal arrest for so-called immigration violations. Yet seeing Osho celebrating each night with his people was evidence of pure life affirmation.

On the third evening after the extraction, immediately after the White Robe Evening Meditation Meeting, I received a message that Osho wanted a dental session. Once we were gathered in the dental room he told me that the pain in his mouth was terrible, so severe that it was stopping him from sleeping and interfering with his eating and bodily functions. While telling me, his voice was gentle and uncomplaining. From the tone of his voice he could have just as well been speaking of the beauties of the Himalayas.

Looking into his mouth, I saw the wound was open and filled with food debris. The stitches were gone, and the whole bony socket was exposed. The bone was completely bare with the soft gum tissue rolled back. There was no semblance of healing. It was a mess. It seemed that his tissues had lost their capacity to heal and regenerate. My worst fears had materialized. The wound was acutely infected, though localized, but in a man with a diminished healing response due to diabetes and asthma, it could easily and quickly become a life-threatening systemic infection.

I cleaned the wound carefully, and placed locally-acting antibiotic in the socket's depth, along with my favorite pain reducing concoction that I had used for years in similar situations. I loosely re-sutured the wound, and hoped for the best.

Within three hours I was called again. Osho told me the pain was very much worse. It was a dental emergency. I decided to cut away the dead and infected bone in order to produce a clean and newly bleeding socket. In this way we would be back at square one with the best chance of a good healing result. In addition, his doctor, Devaraj, would provide supplemental systemic antibiotics and pain relieving medication. The operation took over an hour and proceeded without a hitch.

Two hours later, in the middle of the night, Osho called me again. *"The pain is much, much more terrible."*

I was at a complete loss. Surgically, I had done all I could do. Devaraj and I could now only wait for the antibiotics and painkillers to kick in.

Over the course of the next days, two or three times each day I was called. I would renew the dental dressing and clean the wound. He was in severe, undiminishing facial pain and I felt utterly helpless.

At each dental session, Shunyo, Devaraj, Nityamo, and Anando were present, and Osho continued his masterly games. Now, he concentrated on Shunyo and Anando. His ego-blasting methods reminded me of the times in Rancho Rajneesh when he had continuously accused me of wanting him to stop speaking, and of interrupting him. This time it was Shunyo and Anando who were receiving the masterly bombshells designed to dissolve their egos

In order to discuss the clinical situation and get

expert dental feedback, I was in regular daily communication with Dr. Darius Modi, the urbane, greatly respected, maxillo-facial specialist surgeon in Pune. He confirmed that I was doing all that could be done to ease Osho's pain.

But despite our best efforts it got worse. Osho stopped coming to the Evening Meeting. His eating and drinking were severely affected, along with his sleeping. Although his complete physical balance was in chaos, each time I saw him he looked serene. His voice was soft and gentle. Osho had often told us that our fundamental nature is not rooted in the body-mind. *"We are not the body, the mind or the emotions. Human beings are rooted in existence itself. We are part of the beyond, but we have forgotten our roots."* Osho's demeanor and communication clearly showed the existential truth of his words.

Devaraj and I were puzzled and alarmed. Osho's underlying diabetes meant that any localized infection could spread quickly throughout his body. We had to control the infection but we didn't know the specific bacteria causing it. We took daily tissue swabs and blood samples hoping to identify the infectious agent.

Each day I would travel to three Pune pathology laboratories, leaving a sample at each. I quickly became a regular customer. Why three labs?

Ruefully, we had found that the accuracy of each laboratory was inconsistent, leaving their individual results open to doubt. To get some kind of consensus we had to put the three results together and base our clinical decisions on the two that tallied most closely. Often they were very different. Time and again during those days of helplessness, Osho would say, *"Devageet, you can do it ... but you are missing something."*

Avirbhava, Osho's room caretaker, knew little of medicine, and had a highly-strung disposition. The sight of blood, teeth and surgical instruments appeared to make her jittery and anxious. Seeing our concern and noting our helplessness boosted her nervousness dramatically.

She shared her alarm with her close friend, Yogi. Yogi was an American doctor, a specialist in pathology. He in turn shared his worry with Kavisha, a mature Jewish-American woman of considerable wisdom, great chutzpa and undeniable charisma. Between Yogi, Kavisha and Avirbhava, the collective attitude to illness was to immediately summon the best specialist that money could buy.

As the days passed without any relief from his pain, the emotional pressure of Osho's situation on Avirbhava was reaching boiling point. On more than one occasion, having heard Osho telling me that I was missing something, she had urgently whispered to me, "Why don't we just fly in a specialist from the United States?" She told me, "Kavisha is in the States having her own dental work carried out by a fantastically qualified specialist. We could fly him in."

Knowing Kavisha was no ordinary woman, it was

plain to me that her dental specialist was unlikely to be an ordinary specialist. Avirbhava told me that he only treated very special people. His patients included heads of government, kings and queens, global leaders of industry, warlords, film stars of the first echelon, dictators, drug overlords, Mafia godfathers, and other equally special people.

Hearing of his greatness, I had nodded numbly. Clearly Kavisha's dentist was the best that money could buy. In my severe clinical impasse I felt at the very bottom of the scale of dental excellence, despite continual support from Doctor Modi. I would be only too glad to invite the great man to India, but I told her that only Osho made such decisions. When Avirbhava had suggested it to Osho, he had declined saying, *"No, there's no need to fly in a specialist. Devageet is doing perfectly well, but he is missing something."*

In my dilemma, I had phoned a number of dental specialists around the world, and although they were helpful, it was plain that they were not keen to share their expertise with an unknown caller from India. And it is no easy thing to diagnose and advise over the telephone. In the strange world of medicine, advice, though sincerely given, could be easily misunderstood and become grounds for later litigation.

As Osho's health deteriorated, only those in his personal household knew of the seriousness of the situation. His privacy was paramount, and nothing was more private than his state of health. Rumors among sannyasins moved at the speed of light, and the accuracy of their content was usually inversely proportional to their velocity. Kavisha was evidently kept informed daily of Osho's condition by Avirbhava and Yogi.

I telephoned Kavisha's specialist in America, telling him the situation. He quizzed me deeply and offered several different diagnoses, each one more terrible than the last. He told me in no uncertain terms that we should stop the antibiotic cover we had devised, and that Osho should immediately be placed on a mega-dosage penicillin regime for a minimum of six months. That was the only way, he emphasized, that we could hope to prevent the inevitable spread of infection that might, at best, cause him to lose his jawbone and most of his face, and at worst create a generalized septicemia that would undoubtedly kill him. My already deep anxiety was not diminished by his advice.

Devaraj and I decided that massive long-term penicillin therapy, without first ascertaining whether the causative agent was sensitive to it, was not a good idea. Devaraj argued convincingly that penicillin in high doses would have its own side effects on Osho, and without isolating the organism, we had no way to know if the infection would be reduced by the huge amounts of penicillin. And anyway, the antibiotics we were using were more powerful with a broader spectrum than penicillin. Changing the medication without having found the offending organism did not make clinical sense.

Osho himself was not enthusiastic to receive long-term penicillin therapy without there being a very good reason. His previous experience with penicillin had not been an unqualified success.

When I told Kavisha's specialist of Osho's response, he was outraged that we, his medical team, would listen to the opinion of a patient. "Hey, you guys! Who the hell is the doctor in your outfit? Who is supposed to know the best course of treatment, you guys or the patient?" His point was valid, but not in the world of Osho and his disciples. How to explain to the great man that this was a mystery school and not Mount Sinai Hospital?

It is true that the usual relationship between doctor and patient is not one of equals. The patient gives precedence to the expertise of the man in the white coat. The doctor is the one in power and control.

In Osho's case, the question of power and control was never an issue. His medical team always gave precedence to him. We informed him, and he decided which option to choose. Osho always took responsibility for himself. He is the Master, no matter what situation prevails. As his medical team, we walked a tightrope stretched between our medical training and the master-disciple love we shared with him. I was destined to find out more about this particular tightrope.

Osho was more than our patient, he is our spiritual master, and we are his disciples. This was a difference that made all the difference. Although professionally attentive to each clinical situation, we were also very alert to the instructions we were receiving from Osho, knowing that he was using the clinical scenario for his own work of bringing us into a higher state of consciousness. It was a game of mirrors. It might appear to be dentistry, but the doctors were also on the operating table.

To an outsider, giving precedence to the patient seems like madness. But a Master uses each situation for his alchemy of transformation. Our professional knowledge, and other symbols of clinical power, became mere ingredients placed in the crucible of events. The abrasion between professional knowledge and the master-disciple trust provides the heat that burns away the apparent and exposes the real.

Our different worlds made my communication with the special specialist difficult and delicate. I told him that Osho was in charge of his own treatment and that Osho made his own clinical decisions based on accurate information.

My explanation brought his torrent of words to a shocked halt. I heard a muttered, "Jesus!" But he swiftly gathered himself before barking a request for Osho's complete medical history going as far back into his childhood as we had records, "and fax it to me as quickly as you can," he ordered.

That evening and most of the night I spent gathering the material he had requested and typing a fax of several pages. I stumbled into bed at 5:00 a.m.

A few minutes later I was awakened by a knock on my door. "Osho wants to see you." It was Avirbhava's voice. I told her to pass on the message to Nityamo, while I quickly threw on a thin robe and hurried into the dental room to switch on the airconditioners. It took an hour for the special AC to cool the big room sufficiently for Osho's comfort.

The dental room was in utter darkness as I entered. Dimly I caught sight of my reflection in the polished granite walls with their long, inset mirrors. Suddenly I was startled into awakening; there, standing in the darkness was Osho, looking at me.

Shocked, I raised my hands in namaste. His slight figure, almost lost in the depths of his night robe, seemed insubstantial. He returned my greeting, saying, *"Geet, I have not been able to sleep. I could not find the light switch. Sit down, I have something important to tell you."*

Chapter 14
Osho's Last Dental Drama: Act IV
Osho's Akashic Transmission:
'Your Teeth Contain Memories Back To The Beginning Of Evolution.'

I quickly switched on the lights, seated him in the dental chair, and then sat on the floor at his right side.

"Shall I get a notebook?" I asked bemused.

No, just listen carefully. No need to write anything down. Let it go deep. You will remember what you need to remember. During these last few days the pain in my teeth has been terrible. I have not been able to sleep. Lying in my bed for hours, for the first time in my life I have thought about teeth. Who normally thinks about teeth, except dentists, and madmen like me?

What I am about to tell can prove to be of great significance to you and to every true seeker. I do not think it has ever been told before, perhaps not even known. Maybe in some ancient mystery school it may have once been known. It is possible that this information has been hidden, more likely it has been lost. I have never come across it before, and I have read all the esoteric books possible.

Listen carefully, and when I have finished you will put it out as a world press release. I followed the pain in my teeth down through the bones of my jaw into the middle of the chest. The pain from the teeth appeared like lines of fire, lines of light leading to a place in the center of my chest. The place in my chest appeared as a ball of light. The ball of light is connected by a river of light to a much vaster light, like a huge sun, outside of the body. That sun is the collective unconscious mind of the whole human race. It seems that our teeth connect each individual to the whole collective unconsciousness of humanity.

I am speaking of the real human collective unconsciousness mind, not the collective of Carl Gustav Jung. Jung's collective unconscious mind is merely the collective common ancestry of mankind's myths and legends. It is a kind of mental mythological history that has been left behind by humanity on its long journey.

No, the real human collective unconscious that I am speaking of is much vaster, much older; it is the record of humanity's biological evolutionary history. The real human collective unconscious mind is the millions of years of Man's experiential memories, stored and recorded as a code in the DNA in each cell of the human body. It is our human biological collective inheritance. The record of the path that humanity has followed during the whole long journey of evolution is the true human collective unconscious mind.

And our body remembers! Memories are stored in the DNA of each cell. Each human body contains memories. It remembers our evolutionary history back to the beginning of time, long before there were human beings.

Devageet, it seems that each person's teeth are their individual link, their evolutionary link to existence itself; the teeth hold memories connecting each person to the human collective unconscious mind. The teeth of each person contain a complete record of all their memories back to the time when he was a monkey, maybe before. The teeth are a personal akashic record of everything that has happened to an individual during their whole evolution.

And it continues, the teeth record all that is happening, even now. It does not stop. It is happening now. Memories stored in teeth? It may seem a little strange, but it is not. Crystals are able to store much information. Your computer chips store millions of pieces of information. Just a small computer chip can hold so much. Yes, the enamel in the teeth is made of millions of tiny crystals, and each one is like a computer chip, and there are millions of them. A computer chip may be very small but it can hold millions of facts, and in your teeth you have millions of crystals. The brain is a bio-computer, and the teeth contain all its memories, from today going back through millions of years of evolution.

If the teeth could be used rightly, Devageet, treated in a new way, to release the memories they hold, it is possible to find the roots of many diseases there. Much of the madness that affects people can be treated through the teeth. If we knew how to use the teeth rightly the madhouses would be empty: Just taking out the right tooth, just taking out the right nerve, cleaning out the infection in the teeth and the gums can clean the whole body and the mind. Working with the teeth is very healing for the whole person.

I found that certain of my teeth contain memories with my mother, my father, my family, other relatives, and friends. Sometimes within the same tooth the different root nerves are connected to different people and different events. This one –(he tapped his lower right first molar)– has memories of my mother.

This is of great significance for meditators because the roots of all human conditionings are there; physical, emotional, mental and other deeper conditionings. The ancientmost biological male and female conditionings are found in the teeth. The oldest relationship conditionings can be found there.

The deepest, ancientmost conditioning for a woman is the need to be needed. It is the need to be needed that interferes with every female seeker's deep meditation. I will have to explain a little more:

Most Masters from the past were men; or rather, they had a male body, but a true Master is neither man nor woman. He has gone beyond gender. He has gone beyond any kind of biology. A Master has gone beyond any relationship; and not just with women; any relationship, friendship, mother and father, what to say of what you call love?

The Master is utterly alone. There is not even the possibility of relationship, not even with the mother, the father, and friends. It may be a little difficult to understand for you, but you can try. You may not understand today, but maybe tomorrow, or the next day ... and there are only seven days in the week.

The Master, and any enlightened being, has gone beyond mind, and the mind is the ego. It is the mind, with all its conditioning, that contains all ideas of relationships and dependencies. They are all rooted in our ancient biological memories. In enlightenment the relationship with one's own self also disappears. It too is a type of relationship.

The Enlightened One has no mind in this sense. All conditionings have gone, and gone forever. When the ego finally disappears there is nobody, no self. The Master has cut the roots of biological bondage. For him all unconsciousness has disappeared. All that remains is the nothingness that Buddha calls 'anatta'.

Enlightenment means that nothing stands in the way between existence and the Enlightened One. He stands alone and naked before existence. In a certain sense he is no more. He has dissolved into the void, into Existence. His trust is immense. His ego has dissolved into his trust. What was ego is now trust. He has become trust. He has become love. There is no ego in the way. He has dissolved into the beyond, into Existence itself. He is a continuity with Existence. For the Enlightened One there is total discontinuity with the mind and all that went before. The past has been completely dropped. Relationship is utterly impossible.

The need to be needed means that every woman seeker, deep down, wants the Master to be her personal property; she calls it love. It feels like deep love but it is biological conditioning at the deepest level. You can see it with my closest devotees, though they are not aware of it. She wants the Master to be her lover, according to her biological conditioning. And it is simply not possible.

The Master's love is not the love that comes from the body. It is no longer the chemistry of biology, of hormones, of neurochemicals in the nervous system ... no! The Master's love is not that at all; it cannot be. He is no longer the body. Love is the law of Existence. The Master has merged with Existence. Love is the very stuff Existence is made of, but it is far beyond what human beings call love.

It is very difficult for a woman disciple to be with a Master because her whole conditioning is calling for 'love,' to be needed. More than anything else she needs to be needed. And most Masters are in male bodies. This is because the male energy is more outgoing; it is more able to withstand the tremendous strains on the physical body when enlightenment happens.

Throughout history most Masters that we know of have been men. But existence is always utterly balanced and fair. As many women as men have become enlightened. There is no question about it, but their bodies have died. Becoming a Master is not the same as becoming enlightened.

In a certain way enlightenment is simple, but living as an enlightened being is altogether different. It takes tremendous effort to stay in the body. And when you add the dimension of being a Master, it becomes even more complicated. Not only is it physically arduous to stay in the body, but the masses of humanity want to kill you! They do not want anybody to remind them that their lives are pointless, meaningless and unfulfilled, full of suffering, misery and pain. They do not want to hear about enlightenment. It is easier for them to kill the Enlightened One.

In a certain way being a Master is an existential joke.

Last night I found out that this is why the old-style Masters did not have women in their communes of seekers. It was too difficult. The biological conditioning of their female disciples made it too complicated. All my life I had believed that Buddha and Mahavira were, in a certain way, cowardly. I had always believed they had excluded women from their Sangha because of the social pressures, the difficulties with the priests and the politicians.

Last night, after I discovered the biological conditioning in the teeth, I went to speak to Buddha and Mahavira.

Buddha said he knew of the deep female conditioning and, at that time, in his time, there were no methods available for him to work with it. He told me he had to wait 2500 years, for me. In Buddha's day there was no psychotherapy, no psychological methods for exposing the deepest layers of conditioning. Buddha had to work with men because at least their conditioning was available to the methods of that time, for women his methods were less effective.

I spoke to Mahavira too. He said the same. I told him that for my whole life I had thought he and Buddha had been cowardly in keeping women out of their communes. He laughed. He told me that the priests and the politicians were not the problem at all; they were simple compared to women. It was the deepest biological conditioning in the female that forced him to make the decision to not include women among his commune of seekers. He told me that his simple methods were too primitive to release women from their conditioning. Like Buddha, Mahavira said he had been waiting, all the Masters have been waiting, for a man like me who has all the psychological methods to help women to drop their conditioning and be free.

This is why I have the psychotherapy groups. They do the work of destroying your conditioning, of wiping you clean. Their methods can make you aware of your conditioning very quickly. Now I will create a group which will liberate women from the need to be needed. A women's liberation group; the real liberation! The so-called Women's Liberation Movement is not liberating at all. It has not liberated a single woman. It is merely the foolish attempt of political women to behave more like men.

The real liberation, for women, and for men, is the liberation from the past, from the rotten old diseased mind that keeps the whole of humanity, men and women, in bondage. And at its very root the bondage is biological. For the ultimate transformation to happen the biological bondage must be broken.

I am not afraid of the priests and the politicians, not a bit! I am not afraid of anybody. What can they do to man like me? I have attained to all the blessings that are possible for anybody. The most they can do is to kill my body, and I am not the body ... so they are helpless against me. This is why they fear me.

I will go on doing my work for as long as existence wants it to happen. And I do it totally. And when existence says, 'No more,' I shall immediately be gone, without even a backward glance. I have loved it all, and my love will continue, but when it is finished, it is finished. I neither started it, nor will I end it. My whole life, every breath I take, is in the hands of existence.

This is why all the governments, all the religions, all those who want to destroy the individual – and it is only the individual who is the real humanity – are against me. I am not afraid of them, and they all control humanity through fear. Politicians and priests are the whole repressive past of humanity. I am the beginning of a whole new way for humanity. I herald the New Man, a total freedom unto himself.

A man like me is a threat to all the priests and politicians, to their whole effort. It has always been thus. An enlightened Master has to stand against the whole rotten past of humanity. He is the future; they are for the past. They sacrifice the whole living future of humanity to the dead past.

The real future of humanity is not in the hands of governments or the big organizations. It cannot be. It is up to each individual to realize their hidden potential, their hidden splendor. When human beings stop being followers, stop being sheep, then they are ready to claim their real inheritance as individuals. Every individual has the potential to be a Buddha.

Nobody can save anybody. All your so-called saviours are bogus! You can only save yourself, and nobody else. The most anybody can do is to fan the flame that rests in the heart of every human being. It is there, waiting. It can wait forever. It knows nothing of time. That flame in your heart is eternal. It is the eternal flame of longing for the Universal, for the vast emptiness of Infinity. Only enlightenment can fulfill that longing.

This discovery about teeth can be of immense help to every meditator because the teeth can be used to bring consciousness and awareness to the oldest human conditionings. It is these ancient conditionings, our deepest unconscious, that are the invisible barriers to meditation. It is our biological bondage.

Devageet, you will find a way for the teeth to release their memories, to open the door for human beings to go beyond their biological bondage. Meditation can only reach the depths where authentic transformation happens when it breaks through the biological bondage.

And meditation is the only way to the ultimate transformation for a human being. The memories are locked in the deep layers of the collective unconscious mind, and the teeth can be used as the key. With awareness the true seeker can bring all the unconscious memories in the teeth to consciousness. This will be a tremendous breakthrough in their meditation. This will enable people to go deep enough in their meditation for the real transformation to happen.

You may not know it Devageet, but most people who try to meditate cannot go very deep because their biology pulls them back. It acts as a barrier. Meditation is from the stars, and biology is from the earth. Our biology, like all biology, is programmed for the survival of the species. It knows nothing of the stars. It knows only the earth. Biology has four million years of evolution behind it, and each person has that whole program for survival written in his and her very cells.

Biology is blind, it pulls you to the earth. Biology knows nothing of higher consciousness. Meditation is from the stars. Meditation can take you home, it has eyes. But it takes an exceptional meditator to overcome the gravitational pull of thousands of years of biology. Your higher consciousness has a force too; it is levitation. As gravity pulls you downward, levitation pulls you upwards. Meditation brings the upward vertical movement to your consciousness. There is always balance in existence.

Normally, the scales are weighted in favour of biology. What are ten years, fifteen years of meditation, against the four million-year inheritance of biology? Your biology is your bondage.

But it is possible – for the exceptional people almost anything is possible. The Masters, those few immense peaks of human consciousness, by their spiritual achievement, they have shown throughout human history that meditation and enlightenment is possible. The Masters are the proof. And Meditation is the only possibility, the only door through which enlightenment can enter. There is no other way.

For the meditator it is the attachment to the body-mind that is their biological bondage, and until this attachment is dissolved it is too difficult for an ordinary person to go deep enough in their meditation for enlightenment to happen.

The older religions knew something of this but their priests, being unenlightened, have taken a wrong step, made the wrong interpretation. All religions are formed by unenlightened people. No enlightened being forms a religion. It is the followers that form the religions. The religious traditions all try to fight biology. They tell you to renounce the body, to abuse it, and torture it into submission, to force it to surrender. This is sheer madness. Who is the abuser? Who is the renouncer? It is the ego, the personality-self, the mind that has been conditioned into the religious belief system. It is a terrible mistake to fight with the body and the mind; in fact, it is the opposite of meditation, it strengthens the ego. Perhaps that is the real goal of organized religions.

Out of a thousand people who try to meditate, one may succeed, may go deep enough, may reach the abysmal depths where enlightenment can happen. For the others their biological bondage is too much.

Out of a thousand who manage to really meditate, one may get enlightened. And remember, meditation is the only possibility for enlightenment.

Out of a thousand who get enlightened, one may

live ... because the impact of higher consciousness on an unprepared body-mind is too much. The higher vibration of enlightenment puts tremendous strain on the physical body. Most people die when they get enlightened. The vibration of higher consciousness is usually too much for a human body-mind that has not been prepared. But with the right preparation it is possible for a human body to live many years after enlightenment. Gautamma the Buddha, he managed 42 years. Mahavira, he also lived long. It is possible. If it is possible for one, it is possible for all.

Out of a thousand Enlightened Ones who manage to live, one may speak. What can one say about the immensity that has happened? Where can one find the words? And who will understand? Who bothers to listen? Most ordinary people think the Enlightened Ones are mad. It is a strange paradox; in an insane world the few who attain to sanity are regarded as mad, and the truly mad, those who are the maddest, become the leaders, the rulers, the presidents and the popes.

Out of a thousand enlightened beings who live and speak, one may be a Master.

A Master is a rare individual, the rarest. He is the rarest, most valuable jewel for humanity. Why? Because the Master has been prepared by existence, through thousands of lives, so that after enlightenment, for his remaining years, he can help others find their own inner light. It is the Master's own light that will brings home to others that they too can find the way to their own enlightenment. And without enlightenment your whole life is wasted. Enlightenment is the only real fulfillment possible. Other than enlightenment everything else is a false coin, it has no value.

The old way to enlightenment is a bullock cart method; it is too slow, too arduous for modern people. If this poor suffering humanity is to survive there needs to be a better way, a quicker, a more modern way to enlightenment, a way which is available to more people, a way which will enable people to live when they become enlightened. Now, everybody wants things to be quick, even enlightenment. Maybe they are right, because there is not much time left.

Humanity needs living enlightened individuals if it is to survive. They will raise the collective consciousness of the whole world. And it doesn't need many; two hundred enlightened ones will bring a total transformation to humanity. Two hundred enlightened beings will be enough for humanity to drop its suicidal past and herald the dawn of the New Man.

And even now it may be too late. The priests and the politicians are bringing mankind to a global suicide. This whole beautiful planet may die because of their insanity. Individual seekers need to find a new way to break through their ancient biological bondage, to help their meditation to go deep enough for the ultimate transformation to happen.

And, Devageet, there is a way. You will find a way. It is no accident that existence has shown me this at this time. You will find a way, using the teeth to release their memories and to dissolve the biological bondage that holds people tethered.

The teeth are the key to open the door to each person's akashic record, which goes back to the beginning of evolution, even before the time when man was still a monkey.

Devageet, using the teeth you will find a way to release those memories to consciousness, to help people to become aware of their roots into existence. Using the teeth in this way will be of immense help for every meditator. First, it will strengthen a person's body to withstand the impact of the energy of higher consciousness, to live after enlightenment happens; and second, it will enable the person's meditation to go deep enough for authentic transformation, for enlightenment to become a real possibility.

But remember, no therapy can make people enlightened. The most any therapy can do is to remove the barriers to meditation. And by using the teeth in this way you can bring awareness to even the ancient conditionings buried deep in the collective unconscious mind.

It may be for the first time that this information about teeth has been made available to humanity. Existence is strange; who knows why it has chosen this moment. And to a dentist! Maybe it is because time is so short.

Devageet, send this information to the world's press agencies. Make a news bulletin and release it to the world. They need to know. What they will do with the information will depend on their state of consciousness; it is not your concern what they will do, you simply put it out."

The press release was sent out as directed. A few newspapers the next day carried a small paragraph: "Guru Speaks of Man's Monkey Molars."

AUTHOR'S NOTE: Osho spoke these words to Devageet in October 1989. They were written, as recalled, on February 18, 2001

Chapter 15
Osho's Last Dental Drama: Act III
Almost Meeting A Remarkable Man

The next day, during the now regular morning dental session, as I was cleaning and irrigating Osho's painful, non-healing dental wound, he suddenly said to Avirbhava, *"When you go to the bathroom you can phone Kavisha and tell her there is no need."* She was sitting holding Osho's feet, and his words clearly startled her.

I had no idea what he was referring to, and judging by the look of astonishment on Avirbhava's face, she was equally surprised. But her reply suggested that although the toilet may have not been in her mind, she knew what Osho was referring to when he mentioned Kavisha.

"But Osho, she is on the plane. At this time she will be almost landing in Singapore," Avirbhava replied.

Osho said quietly yet firmly, *"When you go out you can phone the plane and tell her, no need."*

Avirbhava quickly left the dental room and I continued his dental treatment.

A few minutes later she returned, saying, "I phoned the plane and Kavisha told me they are about to land in Changi airport and they can be in Pune in a few hours. She is asking whether you are saying that there is no need for the specialist to come to Pune, and, if that is so, does it include her?"

Osho replied softly, *"Phone her in the airport in Singapore and tell her that there is no need to come to Pune. She and her dental specialist can return to America on the next plane."*

This was the first time I knew that Kavisha and her specialist were en route to Pune. Evidently Kavisha had taken matters into her own hands and persuaded her dental specialist to come to see Osho, but without having first asked him. I guessed that Avirbhava had told Osho of the plan as she brought him into the dental room.

I later learned that Kavisha, when her anxiety over Osho's dental condition reached critical mass, had persuaded her dental specialist that he must come to Pune immediately. She had evidently managed to take command of his passport and arrange an emergency visa for him. She had issued instructions to his clinical staff to cancel all his patients for the next few days, as well as informing the hospitals he attended as consulting surgeon of his impending absence.

Kavisha was a woman of rare and compelling resources who, having determined that the situation in Pune required an incisive decision, had stepped into the dental breech. She did what she felt was the best thing for Osho, but she not reckoned with the Master himself. From the outset of this dental crisis, Osho had made it plain that he wanted no outside specialists involved.

Avirbhava left the dental room to again phone

Kavisha in Singapore. On her return she asked, "Kavisha is confused, she is asking again, do you mean that she should also not come to Pune? She said that she could come if you want her to."

Osho waited a few moments before saying, *"Tell her there is no need. She can return to L.A. and finish her dental treatment."* Then he added, *"Kavisha loves me too much. She is worried about my health."* He chuckled softly before adding, *"Devageet is doing perfectly well, but he is missing something."*

I didn't know whether to laugh or cry. I felt completely loved and supported, and utterly helpless too as I continued taking care of the wound.

Later the same day Yogi, Avirbhava's friend, phoned me saying, "Devageet, you've got to do something, Kavisha's specialist is having a nervous breakdown! They're back in L.A. He is furious with her. He is threatening to sue her, saying that never in his whole life has he been treated in such a way, and he has never been so humiliated. He is refusing to meet or speak with anybody, and refusing to work. He locked himself in the bathroom and wouldn't come out, not even to speak with his wife. Kavisha is freaked out. Devageet, you must do something!"

"Yogi, be reasonable, what can I do? He is in L.A., and I'm in Pune. If he is not even speaking to his wife how could I speak with him? I have my hands full without having a dental prima donna on my back," I said.

"Look, you have to get Kavisha off the hook. She went out in space to get her hands on this guy's passport. God alone knows how she did it. But she did. She practically kidnapped the guy! She probably told him that she was bringing him to Pune to see the greatest living Master in the world, and when they were almost here …" At this point Yogi's voice became almost a shriek. "He was told there is no need. No fucking need! I can't believe it! Fuck man, she was practically landing in Changi airport when she gets this message! It's a wonder she didn't die on the spot! Can you imagine how this guy must have treated her? Can you imagine what she had to deal with, on the flight back to L.A.?"

My fertile imagination could only conjure up a scene in which Woody Allen encounters the archetypal Jewish mother. But it was obvious that Kavisha had brought the situation onto herself.

"Look Yogi, I can imagine a whole scenario, but how does that help? How can I do anything to help her, even if I wanted to, from the other side of the planet? I can feel in my guts, this is Osho at work. He has created this device to work on you, on Avirbhava, on Kavisha, on me, and even on Kavisha's dental wunderkind."

"Devageet, what are you talking about? We need to get real. The guy's in a crisis! You can at least talk to him. Maybe you can say something that will get him out of the toilet and get Kavisha off the hook. Look, I managed to get a list of L.A. phone numbers where you might be able to reach him. Please try, it's an emergency," he beseeched.

"Another dental emergency," I thought, "that's all I need," as I noted down the multitude of digits Yogi was reading out.

Sitting on my bed in Lao Tzu House later that night I phoned the numbers in sequence, without any answer... until the last. A woman answered, and hearing my request, told me the doctor was incommunicado. "He is speaking to nobody."

I told her that I was phoning from India, and before I could finish she interrupted, saying, "You! You of all people! You have a nerve! Of all the people in the world you're probably the last person he wants to speak to."

There was something utterly hilarious about this whole affair: Here I was, having a row with an unknown woman half a planet away, who was protecting an equally unknown husband who was sitting in a toilet in a monumental sulk over a dental event that had not happened. How could I take this thing seriously? It was a joke.

Suddenly I heard a male voice in the background gruffly asking why she was getting so excited. I heard a muffled exchange, and a man's voice spoke on the phone. I recognized the voice. It was him, the special specialist.

"What the fuck do you want!" he shouted angrily, "I want you to know that nobody, and I mean fucking nobody! Has ever treated me in this way. I see the biggest names in Hollywood. I see the biggest names in business. I am a very important man. I am at the top of my fucking profession, but I have still got a heart. Kavisha really touched me. She was crying to me. I was touched by her sincerity. I must have been fucking mad! I allowed myself to be practically kidnapped and put on a plane to fucking India. India of all places! Who needs to go to India? But I did it for Kavisha. She was crying, I opened my heart to her. I should have known better. I allowed her to cancel my whole work schedule just so she can get me to see her spiritual Master. And then! I could not fucking believe it! In the fucking plane we get a phone call! In the fucking plane!" He was momentarily lost for words as he recalled the dreadful scene.

He continued, "And what was the message? No fucking need! What in God's name is that supposed to mean? I had been flown around half the world, to only be told, 'No need!' I could not believe it. I still can't believe it. I have never been so humiliated in my whole life."

He went on in this vein for a time, and then realized that I was not saying anything back. I was waiting for him to draw breath, allowing him to off load and express his wounded feelings.

Cooling somewhat, he added, "Okay, okay, I know it's not your fault, at least not directly. What can you do? You poor shmuck, you have to work with this guy all the time. I feel sorry for you."

I replied, saying, "I am not a poor shmuck. And

there's no need to feel sorry for me. Not only that, but working with this man is the greatest thing that has ever happened to me. I am not expecting you to even understand, but I wanted to phone you, to thank you for what you did. You gave me advice. You allowed me to bounce my worries off you. You did what you thought was best. I didn't know you would be shanghaied."

He broke in, laughing. "Yeah, this Kavisha, she's quite a woman. Yeah, it's true. I mean, look, I know the pressures, after all, we're in the same business. Like I said, it's not your fault."

I interrupted him. "You're still not getting it. I don't have pressures, at least not in the way you mean. Osho is not an ordinary man. He is my spiritual Master. I guess he is using this whole situation as a device, a situation for you to look over the edge of your personality and maybe to catch a glimpse of who you are when you are not an incredibly important dental specialist.

I don't know how to say this, but you will never forget what happened to you today. This journey, this whole experience, will stand out in your mind for the rest of your life. You have just gone through a life-changing event."

He was uncharacteristically quiet at the other end of the world. "What in God's name are you trying to say to me?" he finally asked.

I said, "I don't exactly know how to say it, but I can feel it in my guts. Today you almost met Osho. What other man would, or could, create such a situation for you to get a glimpse of yourself, without even meeting you? Your almost-meeting with Osho has a value that you cannot even begin to estimate right now. But let it in. Your heart is open; you trusted Kavisha, and, in a certain way, you trusted Osho too. This whole episode, bizarre though it appears on the surface, has a deeper meaning and significance that will affect your life from this moment on.

I know it sounds mysterious. In fact, the whole thing is a mystery, but we are not dealing with ordinary events here. Osho is an enlightened mystic. Ordinary events become extraordinary when he is involved. There is more under the surface than you or I can see or understand. Here in Pune, it happens all the time, but this is your first contact. You almost met the most remarkable man on Earth. And without knowing how or why, I know you will be deeply affected by it. And what you get out of it is up to you."

I braced myself for another barrage of expletives. But the specialist was special in this way too. He said, "Look, Dave, I can't pretend to know what you're talking about but I can feel your sincerity. You've got heart too. I can feel it. I appreciate your calling me. And you wanna know something? For no good reason I'm feeling better."

Later that night Yogi phoned, saying, "Devageet, what did you say to the guy? You're a genius! He phoned Kavisha right after you called him, and at this moment they are having dinner together at the best place in L.A."

"Yogi, I simply told him he nearly met the most remarkable man on the planet."

Chapter 16

Osho's Last Dental Drama: Act II
Dental Fire Test: Are You My Dentist Or My Disciple?

In September 1989, after a week of intense facial pain from a localized bone infection following the surgical removal of a lower wisdom tooth, Osho's health declined quickly. The wound was not healing. The surgical site, the bony socket where the tooth had been, was exposed and infected. Painkilling drugs and antibiotics were not helping much. He asked for dental sessions two or three times each day and night to ease the pain. I regularly irrigated the socket and dressed the wound, but the pain steadily increased.

"You can do it Devageet, but you are missing something," he would say gently after each session. Asked if he wanted to fly in a dental specialist he said, *"No need. Devageet can do it, but he is missing something."*

Each day I searched, examined, did daily pathology tests, and conferred with Dr. Darius Modi, the local maxillofacial specialist, to no avail. The pain stayed intense. At least the infection was being contained, staying localized, rather than spreading and becoming systemic.

One day, as I was going over and over the clinical situation, I surmised that the intense pain might be radiating from the tooth in front. I guessed that at least part of the pain might be coming from a source other than the infected wound.

I took x-rays but nothing was to be seen, but that was often the case with Osho. He frequently showed symptoms days before the clinical signs appeared. In this case too, it was possible that a miniscule acute infection in one of the nerves inside the tooth in front of the infected socket might be causing at least some of the pain. Such an infection could easily be too small to show on an x-ray, but its painful effects could be extreme. It was a long shot, but I told Osho.

He listened carefully before asking me what would be the treatment if my hunch were true. I told him that I would have to open the tooth, expose the nerve and have a direct look. If my intuition was right, then the infection would be able to be seen directly. Whatever the case, the surgically exposed nerves would require root canal treatment. He nodded and told me to go ahead.

Opening the second permanent molar and locating the hair-thin nerves that radiate from the tooth part into the root was a tricky affair requiring patience and vigilance. I found three nerves as they entered the three roots of the molar. On the tip of one nerve was a tiny ulcerated area. My intuition had been right. I had found the missing causal link creating Osho's terrible pain.

Jubilant, I told him what I had found. He gave the merest of nods. And I then did the best root canal of my life; three sinuous, curling nerves extirpated and their tiny tubular canals cleaned, disinfected, widened, medicated and then accurately filled to the apex.

The root canal took five hours. At its completion I was relaxed and happy knowing I had worked to the limits of my capacity, and the results were beautiful, dentally speaking.

A few hours later Osho called for another dental session. In the sumptuous dental room he said, *"Devageet, the pain is much less, about eighty percent less. Still, something is there, but it is very much better. But a little pain, twenty percent, still remains."*

I was elated. Such a significant pain decrease within a few hours of this complex procedure, in an area of diminished healing response, was brilliant. Osho asked me when I would expect the pain to go completely. I replied saying that it is impossible to accurately predict but since there had been such a dramatic improvement in a short time, I hazarded a guess that the pain would be completely gone within twenty-four hours.

"And, if the pain has not gone in twenty-four hours, what will you do then?" he asked softly.

"We will simply wait until it has disappeared completely," I said.

"And what if it doesn't disappear completely?" he persisted.

I was a little puzzled by his probing. "With such a quick and positive response as we have now there is every possibility that the pain will completely go. But in the remote eventuality that it does not I suppose we would then consider taking out the tooth."

"You know me Devageet, and my time is always now. Take the tooth out now," Osho said.

I was astonished at his request. To attempt another extraction just when there had been such an swift improvement and decrease in his pain seemed unnecessary, and dangerous too. The adjacent tooth socket was still unhealed, open and infected. Osho's request, in the face of an improving situation, was madness. It would double the size of the existing wound for no good reason; and, after all, the pain was eighty percent better.

I attempted to clearly express my opinion and outline the clinical risks to Osho. He listened carefully before saying, *"It is my body, and I know you love me but I want you to take out this tooth. Never act out of fear. I will take full responsibility for what happens afterwards."*

I felt completely stuck. The course of action Osho was requesting was so abundantly, dentally wrong: to put his ailing body through another surgical procedure, especially so soon after the five-hour root canal ordeal of the morning could not be right. And for no good reason: the pain was diminishing! What Osho was requesting was against all surgical principles. It was downright dangerous. It seemed utterly capricious.

But I knew Osho well. He was never capricious, even though it may appear to be so by minds that could not fathom his point of view. I knew that he must have a good reason. But he was asking me to do something dangerous, something completely against my better clinical judgment.

And I desperately did not want to say no to him. I tried again to make my reasons clear. "Your body is not well and you haven't been able to sleep for several nights. With less pain you will now be able to sleep better and you will get stronger. If I were to take this second tooth out, the new wound in addition to the existing socket would become twice as large. The infection from the first wound will probably spread to the second. Your pain is likely to increase, and your body is already weakened from trying to fight off the existing infection. Your diabetes increases your risk of getting a generalized infection from this local infection. Increasing the size of your infected wound increases the risk of a generalized systemic infection, an infection that could become life-threatening. And your immune system is already showing a poor healing response. In addition, I will need to inject the local anaesthetic directly into an already infected area, and that in itself poses great risks of further infection. It could carry the bone infection into the soft tissues of your cheek. Osho, it is surgical madness to extract this tooth; especially now, after such a great root canal." I was pleading for him to listen, to hear my acute concerns for his safety.

He listened attentively, lying still and relaxed on his

Are You My Dentist Or My Disciple?

dental chair. Thick blankets covered his body. Although he liked to breathe cold air, his body needed to be kept warm.

"Devageet. It is no longer your responsibility. It is not your body. It is my body. I know you love and care for me, but it is my body. Take out this tooth. Your dental knowledge is one thing, but I have my own knowledge."

I was in an excruciating impasse, between what I knew to be right, and what he was asking. "I can't do it, Osho. It would be wrong. It would cause more pain, and maybe harm your body even more. I simply cannot do it, Osho." I was becoming frantic, searching for something to add weight to what I was saying. "And you won't be able to chew on this side if I take out this second molar."

I was crying as I said these words. I felt torn in two. Nityamo, his dental nurse, was crying too.

"Devageet, I will never be eating solid food again. And you need not worry. You will not be harming my body. You will not be to blame for what happens to my body. Take out this tooth," Osho said.

Through my tears I said in anguish, "Osho, I cannot do what you ask. It would be wrong. It will cause you more harm than good. It will increase your pain and your infection. What you are asking me to do is wrong. Even though it is your body I cannot and will not do anything to harm this beautiful body." He was close to death and asking me to take him closer to the edge.

He was silent before saying, *"Devageet, I take full*

responsibility for what happens to me. Are you my dentist or my disciple, Devageet?"

With tears streaming I became furious. I shouted at him, "You wicked old man! How dare you say that to me! I cannot do what you are asking. It is wrong! I will not! I will not do anything that will harm your body. I don't care if you throw me out of the commune! I don't care if I never get enlightened! I don't care if all my years of seeking are thrown away. I will not take out this tooth and risk hurting you. And, you're wrong to force me to make this choice!" My words and my tears were wrung from my heart.

This agonizing dialogue went on, with minor variations, for over an hour before Osho finally said, "*Okay Devageet. Enough for today.*"

As always, at the end of a dental session with Osho, we sat quietly at his side. The silence today was especially profound. My heart was hurting as it pounded. I had said no to my beloved Master and my heart was breaking.

He left the dental room, smiling a little, as serene as ever, namasteing each of us in turn.

I was shaking as I left the dental room. As a dentist I knew I had made the right decision. As a disciple I had refused my Master, and I was in pain. Right and wrong had no place in my feelings. The dentist was undeniably right. The disciple was in agony, having no guidelines other than a love that could not be forced to act against itself.

Was I his dentist or his disciple? The question tore me apart.

Dr. Modi, when I told him of the events of the morning, was emphatic in his support of me. "Your root canal is a work of art. How do you manage to do such good work with such a man?" he asked as I showed him the x-rays. "This root canal is one hundred percent. It could not be better. And the reduction in the pain shows that your clinical judgment was right. Nobody would say that you are wrong. You made the right dental decision."

His words supported what I already knew. But they did not touch the agony in my heart. "Darius," I asked, "if I am right why do I feel so wrong?" He shrugged. "We must all make painful clinical decisions," he said, trying to find a clinical way out of a spiritual dilemma.

I smiled ruefully, saying, "He is my Master. I know and trust him. He knows more than I can even guess. I feel I have gone against my trust in him by doing what I know to be right." As I spoke, I realized that Osho had exposed the boundary line in me by asking: Are you my disciple or my dentist?

Darius added, "I would have done exactly as you have done in that situation."

I had a sudden flash of insight. "Darius, I have a feeling you will soon be put to that test. It is my guess that he will call you to take out this tooth."

Darius looked shocked. "Why would he do that? You are his dentist, and a bloody good one too. He should be grateful that you have such strong integrity and principles. You stood by your clinical judgment."

Each of his well-meaning words rubbed salt into the raw wound in the very heart of my being. It was true, my principles had been upheld, but my heart's trust was in deep suffering.

I left Dr Modi's dental office in downtown Pune, returning to the ashram. As I entered Lao Tzu House, there was an urgent message waiting for me at the gate-guard's table. I was being requested to bring Darius Modi to Lao Tzu House.

Within minutes I was back in Darius's rooms in Mahatma Gandhi Road. He was surprised, then grew a little pale as I put Osho's request to him.

Dr. Modi had never seen Osho in his professional capacity, although he knew him well through his wife Zareen, who was a long-time disciple. Osho had also showered attention on Dr. Modi's young son, Faroukh, whenever Zareen brought him to discourse. In fact, I realized, Zareen had made the profound life-choice to leave her husband to go to live as a disciple of Osho in his ashram. And now Darius was to meet Osho face to face.

I escorted Darius into Osho's fabulous dental surgery. His eyes grew wide in disbelief. I knew there was no dental room like this on the planet. Darius' own rooms were less than palatial. This surgery was sumptuous above and beyond anything remotely dental. He had never seen a dental room such as this.

We were in India at a time when dental offices were less than tawdry. This was palatial. He was surrounded by marble and mirrors. There were five other people there, robed and reverent, waiting. Dr. Modi too revered Osho. He did not know what was going to happen. He was very nervous. He was awed and silent as we stood waiting for Osho to enter.

Osho was dressed in a soft green, loosely hanging robe, immaculate as ever. One would never know from his demeanor that he had been unable to sleep for days, that he had been through a five-hour root canal ordeal in the morning, and an excruciating dialogue with his personal dentist; excruciating to his dentist, that is. He looked relaxed and easy, smiling and radiant as he took my help to enter the dental chair.

Osho looked at Darius with a twinkling, soft expression. Disarmingly, he enquired about Dr. Modi's family, and his health. Modi was charmed and flattered.

Turning the conversation to his dental situation, Osho said that he knew that I had been daily in contact with Dr. Modi during the preceding few days. He asked for his opinion on the root canal completed that very morning.

Darius was full of praise for my work, and emphasizing the diagnostic acumen I had shown in finding the cause of the pain. Then, knowing the situation, he was trying hard, too hard, to portray my dental skills by stressing the remarkable feat of not only finding the cause but also of managing to reduce the pain by eighty percent within hours.

"*It is true,*" said Osho, "*My pain has been reduced by more than half. Devageet has done well. Almost eighty percent has gone, but twenty percent is still there.*"

"By tomorrow it will be completely gone," Modi confidently reassured him.

"*And if not?*" Osho asked softly.

Modi's ordeal was about to begin. I knew the drill. "But it will be gone. If it has reduced by eighty percent in a few hours by tomorrow it will surely be gone."

"*And if it has not gone by tomorrow?*" Osho persisted.

Within minutes poor Dr. Modi was shaking, perspiration beading his balding head. Finally he was forced to admit that as a last resort the tooth would need to be extracted. "*I am a strange man,*" said Osho, "*My time is always now. I want you to take out this tooth now.*"

Dr. Modi said, "I cannot do such a thing. It would be surgically wrong, and if anything happened to such a world famous person as you, my reputation would suffer badly." Modi was on the ropes and frantically looking for the exit.

"*I will give you a letter explaining that I take full responsibility, and that you told me all the risks,*" said Osho quietly.

Modi said, "It is not so easy for a non-clinician to understand, but I will try to make all the implications clear to you, showing that I cannot do what you ask. The risks are too great. Devageet's decision was completely in order, in line with all the surgical principles. I very much respect his integrity."

Osho nodded, *"Devageet's integrity is not the question. It is my body, and I want this tooth out."*

Darius then went through all the clinical problems that a second extraction would create. He explained, as I had done already, the severe risks to an aging diabetic whose health was in poor shape. Dr. Modi said everything that could be said.

In a soft clear voice Osho replied,

It is my body, Dr. Modi, and I take full responsibility for it. You have made your position very clear and I respect it utterly. But I am asking you to take out my tooth, knowing that the root canal has been expertly done, knowing the risks to my body. I know the risks and I am willing to face them. I would like you to take out my tooth. I will take care of your reputation by giving you a handwritten letter explaining how thoroughly you have explained the drawbacks. Nobody will blame you if I suffer as a result of what I am asking you to do for me.

Modi was pale and sweating. Beads of perspiration

on his forehead had become tiny rivulets of anguish. He was trembling. There was nowhere else to go.

"Well ... if you give me the letter." He looked briefly and miserably in my direction, as a last forlorn hope before saying, "But I do not have my instruments here."

"*Devageet has everything you will need. He has bought all the best dental instruments. He will give you what you need. Help him Devageet.*"

Darius's hands were shaking so badly that he could not hold the long local anaesthetic syringe. He tried several times. I heard the needle tanging as it touched the teeth while he was searching for the exact location of the injection site. He took out the syringe, steadying his hand to try once more.

Osho said, "*It is okay. Just let Devageet inject my mouth. He knows it well. He will help you.*"

Darius gratefully handed the syringe to me. I administered the local anaesthetic. While the solution took effect we all sat silently. Modi was visibly shaking.

After a few minutes, I tested Osho's mouth to ensure the extraction site was painless, then indicated to Modi that he could start.

The extraction was swift and clean. Modi was an expert. I stitched the surgical site with two black silk sutures.

As I was finishing, Osho said quietly, "*Devageet, now you take out this tooth.*" He pointed with a slender finger to his lower right canine, an innocent tooth without any clinical history or pathology.

I looked at him for a long moment, before saying, "I will need to inject more anaesthetic, Osho." He nodded his head slightly.

I took out the second tooth feeling no twinges in my integrity, nor were my principles complaining.

Dr. Modi looked on wonderingly. A few moments later, Osho indicated the session was over. I raised the chair. He carefully placed his feet in the simple hand-made sandals he had designed.

The next morning, Osho called for an early dental session. He informed me, *"My pain has almost gone completely."* And as I breathed deeply in relief he added, *"And now, take out these two teeth,"* indicating another two unaffected teeth in the same region.

I did it without a qualm. All my qualms had run for cover, unable to face this new dimension of trust. The disciple now stood where before had been a dentist.

That same evening he called for another session, and said his pain had virtually gone. *"It only comes when Nivedano hits his drum!* [1] *Now, take out these two other teeth."*

In all, during the next few days, I extracted nine teeth from Osho's right jaw. When I again pointed out that it would be difficult for him to chew food on that

---

[1] Each night Nivedano's three explosive drum beats signalled the end of the fifteen minutes of music and silence during the Evening Meeting of The Osho White Robe Brotherhood.

side he said that he would never again eat anything solid.

Osho's behavior had seemed irrational. I was an ordinary, rational, conditioned, professionally-trained person, confirmed in my own self-belief and clinical acumen. Osho's enlightened koan – are you my dentist or my disciple? – brought me to face my divided self.

I was cornered into choosing between the two. As Osho's disciple, I was on a spiritual path, developing awareness through meditation in order to discover the unknown, higher aspects of consciousness, beyond my conditioned mind. As a dentist, I had been trained in special skills. My ego was invested in my knowledge and clinical judgment. Osho's koan faced me with the choice between my trust in Osho as my spiritual master and with myself as a professional.

I had already experienced Osho blasting away at my ego when he dictated the books from the dental chair. That's his work, and he knows it well: to create devices that enable the disciple to break through the false self of the ego to discover the authentic being beneath. He had made it clear: *"Devageet, I will not stop until I crack your concrete skull."*

This was different: he was asking me to risk his life. If we pursued his way of treating his teeth, the balance between recovery and serious consequences could easily be tipped. I was the expert, and I believed my view was correct. Osho challenged my professional judgment, using his body as the arena in which his master's truth encountered my knowledge-belief world of "the expert." I was certain that he would harm his body in ways that he could not know. His behavior challenged my certainty, my truth. It raised the possibility of a greater truth, a truth that I did not know. How could I possibly trust a truth that I did not know? My anguish was rooted in fear of the consequences for his body – his possible death. I knew that his trust has no limits. From his childhood he had shown no fear of death. Osho knows death, he declares it to be the greatest fiction, a lie propagated by various priesthoods as the foundation of their control over believers.

Osho had no fear, but I did, and I felt I had solid clinical grounds. Osho simply trusted himself, his body, and existence itself. I was facing a fearless enlightened master. My master. His trust challenged my whole reason, my mind. Yet I trusted him. I was in a paroxysm of paradox: I also trusted my expertise. For me, death is a reality, and I could not bear to be the cause of his suffering or possible death.

His apparently irrational behavior was moving me beyond my logical, reasonable fear into the unknown vastness of his trust field.

Osho's behavior and my response may easily seem mad to anybody not on an authentic spiritual path. I see it as a supremely loving, higher dimension act that can only take place within the extraordinary bond of trust existing between the master and disciple. Osho used his own body as the crucible for my transformation. The actuality of standing in the fire of his trust was excruciating.

Speaking with Darius Modi after the impasse, I knew my professional self had lost the battle. I had stood for my professional truth by identifying with Osho's physical body, but in doing so I had lost sight of Osho himself, because of my fear of harming him.

Was I his disciple or his dentist? I faced the deeper question: Why was I his disciple? And the answers came flooding into me. Because in his presence I experienced my self in a completely new way. I felt a peace and joy beyond reason or understanding. I encountered previously unknown dimensions of love, trust, gratitude and awareness. Osho had enabled me to experience a new magnitude of being in which the old professional ego had no place.

Subsequent events confirmed Osho to be right in both ways. He recovered quickly and painlessly. The surgical wounds healed with remarkable ease. And my professional certainty was shown as unfounded. The dentist died, along with his well-meant good intentions, and Osho's disciple emerged from the glowing ashes of that fire of transformation. That clinical fire test burned away the dentist, and left only the slightly scorched disciple.

Chapter 17
Osho's Last Dental Drama: Act V
The Last Golden Glimpse

Although his mouth was healing remarkably well, Nityamo and I, along with the other members of Osho personal dental team, Anando, Devaraj, and Shunyo, attended to the healing sockets on an almost daily basis for weeks. Following the nine extractions, Osho never again referred to pain in his teeth. During each session I would bathe and dress the slowly healing wounds, and take care of his remaining teeth.

On one occasion, as I was quietly attending to his teeth, Osho, lying on his back in the dental chair, suddenly asked, *"Geet, do you know the OM sign?"*

I searched my memory and vaguely recalled the Sanskrit script depicting the most ancient of all mantras, Om Mani Padme Hum, the meaning of which – the sound of existence, the song of existence – is one of the meanings of the name Osho had given to me.

"Yes, Osho," I replied.

"I can see it now," he said. *"It appears as a blue OM sign over my third eye. Here, put your finger on it."*

I took off the surgical glove on my right hand and placed my middle finger carefully on Osho's third eye and immediately felt a powerful throbbing vibration.

"Yes, I can feel it pulsing, Osho."

"Nitty, you also put your finger on my third eye. Feel it for yourself," he said.

Nityamo, removing her rubber glove, did the same. "Yes, Osho, I can feel it too," she murmured.

"When the blue OM appears over the Hara it means death," Osho said quietly."

I became afraid and puzzled. Was Osho telling us he was dying? As the thought surfaced I pushed it away telling myself the blue OM was over his third eye, and, for the moment, there was no need to worry. But beneath my efforts at denial I could feel the deeper truth: he was looking so frail, almost ethereal. To my intense relief during the next dental session Osho did not refer again to the blue OM.

On the following day, midway through the session, Osho quietly said, *"The blue OM has moved down. It is now over my Hara."*

I sat very still, scarcely able to think or even breathe. Was Osho saying that he was about to die? Was he going to die here and now in the dental chair? My thoughts were scattered, almost incoherent, leaves driven by the whirlwind of my fear. I sat silently, barely able to comprehend a world, my world, any world, in which I would not be able to see Osho. My breathing became shallow as my fear-driven thoughts forced me to face the implications of his words: that very soon he might not be here, I might not be able to experience the living presence of this wonderful man, my beloved master.

I was dimly aware that Osho must be telling me this for a reason. The heaviness in my heart was blocking my higher awareness. I knew he would not be speaking of his death in this way for no reason. Perhaps he wanted us, me, to be prepared for what he knew was not far off. It was his compassionate way of saying, *"Soon I will be no more. Be ready for the moment. Do not miss it."*

The moment did not come then, it came a few weeks later.

After the blue OM incident my mind avoided any further thoughts of Osho's death. I denied the evidence of my own eyes. I saw him during each evening meeting of the White Robe Brotherhood, daily, visibly, more frail. Still I denied the obvious. My mind continued to avoid the reality that these were Osho's last days.

In the middle of December 1989, Vivek died from an overdose of sleeping pills. Her death came as a shock to everyone in the commune. She had been in a disturbed state of mind for weeks. I had assumed it was due to her turbulent love life. Osho's health, already precarious, took a downturn. At this time he was already spending hours each day in bed sleeping, collecting his fast-depleting energy for the evening meeting with his people.

As December 1989 drew to a close, suddenly, one evening at the commencement of the evening meeting in Buddha Hall, Osho starkly declared that he was being attacked with inaudible sound waves, sound waves beyond the normal range of hearing, aimed to damage his body.

The effect on the huge audience was one of stunned astonishment: one moment we were dancing and celebrating ready for Osho's entry, the next we were utterly astonished and shocked into stillness at his words. His face, as he spoke, was uncharacteristically stern, his large eyes wide and piercing as he gazed to his right side at the hundreds of people gathered there.

He declared to the now silent, white-robed throng, that among us in Buddha Hall there was a small group of people, probably three, who were using sound as a weapon to harm him. A few people giggled nervously, perhaps thinking he was being mischievous. Others knew from his demeanor that this was no joking matter.

During the next days Osho told Shunyo, his caretaker, that there were three attackers, probably members of the same group who had tried to kill him in America. He told her they were using sound waves beyond the normal range of hearing to damage his body. He said that he could hear them, and feel their destructive effect and the pain they caused. He told her that the group had first focused the sound waves on his head, trying to harm his brain and affect his mind. Within a day or two, seeing that he remained lucid and clear despite their worst efforts, they then triangulated the sound waves to focus on his body. His mind could not be damaged by their rays, he explained, because his consciousness was no longer centred in his brain – in an early discourse he had described that since

The Last Golden Glimpse

his enlightenment his consciousness had been released from its biological prison and that it now hovered around his body – but his body was immensely vulnerable. And they were preying on it.

The second night of the sound attacks he had again looked with bright fierce eyes into the audience on his right side. He asked the hundreds of people sitting there to stand up and to change sides; those sitting on the left of the podium should move to sit on the right side. Osho declared in a powerful voice that he could reflect the sound rays back onto the attackers, but he would not allow himself to be provoked into an act of violence even against those who were trying to kill him, even if it meant his own bodily death.

Each night, knowing his suffering, and feeling utterly powerless to stop it, our fear for his safety grew. In their helplessness, the sannyasins grew increasingly anxious, glancing furtively at their neighbors wondering if they might be one of the hidden attackers. The seeds of paranoia were being sown.

During the following days and nights there was no other topic on people's lips. Osho's guards and security team searched throughout the commune premises and around, looking everywhere for suspicious electrical, or other unusual bits of machinery. Some nearby houses were included in our searches. Fear and negative speculation grew thick and fast among sannyasins. Some claimed they too could hear the sound, but their certainty melted into vagueness on questioning. Some even declared that they knew people in the audience who wanted Osho dead. Speculation grew, feeding on our collective fear and concern. Stories of electronic sound transmitters located on waste ground and in neighboring houses further afield were investigated without success.

Rumors of escalating ugliness grew as days passed with nothing to diminish the intensity of fear, and uncertainty about what was happening to our beloved master.

After several days of intense, unbearable anxiety made worse on seeing Osho's evident bodily weakness at each evening meeting, he never again publicly mentioned the attacks. Slowly the sannyasins calmed, but beneath the calm was a terrible knowledge that we could not protect Osho. With each passing day, to cover our fear, we began to assume, to hope, that the threat was over.

By now it was in the early days of January 1990. I asked Shunyo if the sound waves had stopped. With tear-filled eyes she shook her head sadly. "They wait for him to come to White Robe in Buddha Hall each night, and then they attack him; the bloody cowards!" she said angrily. "He told me they were trying to stop him speaking by attacking his mind, but they cannot succeed because his consciousness is not centred there. So now they are attacking his body. Each night in the few minutes he can manage to be with his people in the evening meeting, he has tremendous pain in his liver and abdomen. They are

The Last Golden Glimpse

killing his body." She trembled as she spoke.

"Why did he stop mentioning the attacks when he came in Buddha Hall?" I asked.

"Because it was causing so much fear among sannyasins. These terrible people can use sannyasins' fear. The negative energy of collective fear is being used to strengthen the effect of the attacks on him. His speaking makes it worse. I don't really understand how, but Osho told me that as his people became more and more freaked out, blaming and suspicious of each other, their collective negative energy was helping the attackers. He is in terrible pain. That is why he has stopped speaking about these cowards," she said with quiet vehemence.

Each evening, on entering Buddha Hall, Osho would slowly namaste the whole audience as he made his wavering way to his chair. He sat in silent meditation with us for fifteen minutes during which time the massive audience became merged into a temple of silence, a lake of consciousness without ripples. The consciousness of the master and his people melted into a profound peace beyond mind and body. Then, slowly, with growing difficulty from his weakening body, he would get up from his chair, and once again acknowledge his people while walking slowly backwards, his fine hands steepled in front of his heart in farewell, his body swaying perceptibly with its decreasing vitality. Each evening it seemed that he was saying his final goodbye. I could feel my heart breaking. He no longer danced, but he encouraged us, his people, to celebrate before he arrived and after he had gone: *"Celebration is my message…"*

After he left the podium to return to his bed, the huge audience in Buddha Hall sat meditating together, watching one of his earlier video discourses. Among the thousands of sannyasins, his presence was palpable in their silence.

During this time, knowing I was involved in the security around Osho, people began telling me strange and terrible stories they had heard about secret technologies being used by secret police and intelligence agencies around the world against their perceived enemies. I was given a long newspaper article from "The Age" in Australia, which detailed how a United States oil technician who had brought innovative new methods to Britain had been forced to flee because he had been subjected to mental attacks by unknown people using extra low frequency sound waves as a weapon. The article stated how he had been told that other such attacks had caused the targeted people to commit suicide. The author believed the attacks, in his case, were due to the CIA.

According to various stories and articles it seemed that there was indeed a secret technology, a new range of weapons using ultra-low, and ultra-high frequency, sound waves to kill or maim. But such information only served to emphasise our helplessness and accentuate Osho's vulnerability.

On January 15th, 1990, my birthday, I received a

The Last Golden Glimpse

message from Shunyo: Osho wanted me to take an x-ray of his abdomen.

We met in the dental room. Osho's body looked thin and wasted, yet I felt him powerfully present. I knew from Shunyo that he was sleeping more than twenty hours each day, saving what remained of his physical energy for the few precious minutes in Buddha Hall each evening.

Osho told me that his body had been very much weakened by the sound rays of his attackers. He said there were probably three of them, two men and a woman, sitting in a special formation in order to focus the sound waves and target his body.

There are ancient Yogic practices here in India where people know certain sounds, certain mantras, that can concentrate sound to harm people. But these people attacking me are not Indians. They are the same people who tried to kill me before in America. They could not succeed then, and now they are trying to finish off what they started. They tried poison to stop me speaking but I managed to continue. Now, five years later they are back. They first used their sound rays in Buddha Hall to attack my mind but I am not in my mind. I am a no-mind and their sound had little effect. So they changed their tactics, now they are attacking my body. My poor body has no protection against their rays. Each day it gets weaker. They cannot kill me but they can harm my body. Right now my liver area is hurting very badly. Can you x-ray it?

Sadly, I explained that my dental x-ray machine was probably inadequate because it could only take small films of the teeth and jaws, but we could try.

Amrito found the largest x-ray film we possessed while I jiggled with the dental x-ray machine to widen its beam. I tried to do what Osho was asking. I took a picture of his liver region and then managed to develop the larger film in the dental developing tank that was designed for tiny intra-oral dental films, but the resulting image was blurry and indistinct.

It was the last time I saw Osho in his physical body.

It was 4:30 p.m. on January 19th: I was in my room with my girlfriend when there was an urgent knock on the door. Maneesha, looking pale and stressed, asked if she could use my room phone. I knew she would only ask if there was something unusual happening. Acting as temporary secretary she was phoning the Inner Circle members telling them to immediately come to an extraordinary meeting in Krishna House.

Osho had set up a commune management team of twenty-one people fifteen months earlier, naming it the Inner Circle. He made it clear that their job was to manage the day-to-day running of the commune. I was not in the original selection, but had been asked to join a few months later.

After phoning, Maneesha said, "Geet, you heard what I was telling the others. The meeting is in the Blue Room on Krishna House roof. Can you go there right away?" Before I could ask any questions she vanished hurriedly into the corridor, clearly involved in another important task.

I had felt strangely exuberant most of the afternoon. Despite the turmoil of outer affairs I had been feeling elated for days. There was an inexplicable dance of joy in my heart. Inside I felt euphoric, blissful.

Arriving in the Blue Room, I saw that most of the Inner Circle were already gathered there. The atmosphere was tense and strained. My own euphoria seemed out of place. I sat and waited.

After a few minutes Jayesh entered with Amrito. Looking around briefly to see that we were all present, he said in a firm, though hushed voice, "I guess there's no way to wrap this up. I'll just tell you straight. Osho left his body a short time ago, at about 4:45 p.m."

Stunned, I looked at my watch. It was 5:15 p.m.

Two or three people present began to sob. Jayesh quickly interrupted, "Look, I am going to need all your help. Please don't fall apart just yet. I need you all to help to make Osho's send-off as beautiful as he deserves. This is the last thing we can do for his physical body, let's make it wonderful. He told me exactly how he wants it to happen. He left me detailed instructions for everything, but I need the help of everybody here."

My earlier euphoria had turned to shock on hearing Jayesh's words, but I clearly heard Jayesh's appeal for our help to enable Osho to enjoy his final celebration with his people. As I left the Blue Room Jayesh told me that Osho had requested that I be one of the bearers to carry his body to the burning ghats. In a blur of activity and confused feelings I remember feeling immensely grateful for this last gift from Osho.

The Life of Osho | *a Timeline*

The Life of Osho | A Timeline

December 11, 1931:
Osho is born in Kuchwada, a small village in the state of Madhya Pradesh, central India.
He is the eldest of eleven children of a Jaina cloth merchant. Stories of His early years describe Him as independent and rebellious as a child, questioning all social, religious and philosophical beliefs. As a youth He experiments with meditation techniques.

EARLY YEARS 1931-1953   **EDUCATION 1953-1956**

March 21, 1953:
Osho becomes enlightened at the age of twenty-one, while majoring in philosophy at D.N. Jain college in Jabalpur.

1957:
Osho is appointed as a professor at the Sanskrit College in Raipur.

1956:
Osho receives His M.A. from the University of Sagar with First Class Honors in Philosophy.
He is the All-India Debating Champion and Gold Medal winner in His graduating class.

1958:

He is appointed Professor of Philosophy at the University of Jabalpur, where He taught until 1966. A powerful and passionate debater, He also travels widely in India, speaking to large audiences and challenging orthodox religious leaders in public debates.

UNIVERSITY PROFESSOR 1957-1966

1966:

After nine years of teaching, He leaves the university to devote Himself entirely to the raising of human consciousness. On a regular basis, He begins to address gatherings 20,000 to 50,000 in the open-air maidans of India's major cities. Four times a year He conducts intense ten-day meditation camps.

Late 1960's:

His Hindi talks become available in English translations.

July 1970:
He moves to Mumbai, where He lives until 1974.

April 1970
He introduces His revolutionary meditation technique, dynamic Meditation, which begins with a period of uninhibited movement and catharsis, followed by a period of silence and stillness. Since then this meditation technique has been used by psychotherapists, medical doctors, teachers and other professionals around the world .

MUMBAI YEARS 1969-1974

1970-1974:
Osho – at this time called Bhagwan Shree Rajneesh – begins to initiate seekers into Neo-Sannyas or discipleship, a path of commitment to self-exploration and meditation which does not involve renouncing the world or anything else. Osho's understanding of 'Sannyas' is a radical departure from the traditional Eastern viewpoint. For Him it is not the material world that needs to be renounced but our past and the conditionings and belief systems that each generation imposes on the next. He continues to conduct meditation camps at Mount Abu in Rajasthan but stops accepting invitations to speak throughout the country. He devotes his energies entirely to the rapidly expanding group of sannyasins around Him.

1974 – 1981:

During these seven years He gives a 90 minutes discourse nearly every morning, alternating every month between Hindi and English. His discourses offer insights into all the major spiritual paths, including Yoga, Zen, Taoism, Tantra and Sufism. He also speaks on Gautam Buddha, Jesus, Lao Tzu, and other mystics. These discourses have been collected into over 600 volumes and translated into 50 languages.

In the evenings, during these years, He answers questions on personal matters such as love, jealousy, meditation. These 'darshans' are compiled in 64 darshan diaries of which 40 are published.

POONA ASHRAM 1974 – 1981

1980:

The commune that arose around Osho at this time offers a wide variety of therapy groups which combine Eastern meditation techniques with Western psychotherapy. Therapists from all over the world are attracted and by 1980 the international community gained a reputation as ' the world's finest growth and therapy center.' One hundred thousand people pass through its gates each year.

1981:

Osho develops a degenerative back condition. In March 1981, after giving daily discourses for nearly 15 years, Osho begins a three-year period of self-imposed public silence. In view of the possible need for emergency surgery, and on the recommendation of His personal doctors, He travels to the United States This same year, His American disciples purchase a 64,000-acre ranch in Oregon and invite Him to visit. He eventually agrees to stay in the United States and allows an application for permanent residence to be filed on His behalf.

October 1984:

Osho ends three and one half years of self-imposed silence.

1981-1985:

A model agricultural commune rises from the ruins of the central Oregonian high desert. Thousands of overgrazed and economically unviable acres are reclaimed. The city of Rajneeshpuram is incorporated and eventually provides services to 5,000 residents. Annual summer festivals are held which draw 15,000 visitors from all over the world. Very quickly, Rajneeshpuram becomes the largest spiritual community ever pioneered in America.

1981-1985 cont.:

Opposition to the commune and new city keeps pace with its success. Responding to the anti-cult fervor which pervades all levels of American society during the Reagan years, local, state and federal politicians make inflammatory speeches against the Rajneeshees. The Immigration and Naturalization Service (INS), the Federal Bureau of Investigations (FBI), the Treasury Department, and the Alcohol, Tobacco and Firearms Agency (ATF) are only a few of the agencies spending millions of dollars in taxpayers' money while harassing the commune with unwarranted and fruitless investigations. Similar costly campaigns are conducted in Oregon.

RAJNEESHPURAM 1981-1985

July 1985:

He resumes His public discourses each morning to thousands of seekers gathered in a two-acre meditation hall

September 14 1985:

Osho's personal secretary Ma Anand Sheela and several members of the commune's management suddenly leave, and a whole pattern of illegal acts they have committed – including poisoning, arson, wiretapping, and attempted murder – are exposed. Osho invites law enforcement officials to investigate Sheela's crimes. The authorities, however, see the investigation as a golden opportunity to destroy the commune entirely.

The Life of Osho | A Timeline

October 23rd-28th, 1985:
On October 23rd, A United States federal grand jury in Portland secretly indicts Osho and 7 others on relatively minor charges of immigration fraud. On October 28th, without warrants, federal and local officials arrest at gun point Osho and others in Charlotte, North Carolina. While the others are released, He is held without bail for twelve days. A five-hour return plane trip to Oregon takes four days. En route, Osho is held incommunicado and forced to register under the pseudonym, David Washington, in the Oklahoma County jail. Subsequent events indicate that it is probable that He was poisoned with the heavy metal thallium while in that jail and the El Reno Federal Penitentiary.

THE OREGON COMMUNE IS DESTROYED SEPT.-NOV. 1985

November 1985:
Emotions and publicity swell around Osho's immigration case. Fearing for his life and the well-being of sannyasins in volatile Oregon, attorneys agree to an Alford Plea on two out of 35 of the original charges against Him. According to the rules of the plea, the defendant maintains innocence while saying that the prosecution could have convicted him. Osho and His attorneys maintain His innocence in the court. He is fined $400,000 and is deported from America. Among others, United States Attorney in Portland, Charles Turner, publicly concedes that the government was intent on destroying Rajneeshpuram.

January-February, 1986:
He travels to Kathmandu, Nepal and speaks twice daily for the next two months. In February, the Nepalese government refuses visas for His visitors and closest attendants. He leaves Nepal and embarks on a world tour.

February-March, 1986:
At His first stop, Greece, he is granted a 30-day tourist visa. But after only 18 days, on March 5, Greek police forcibly break into the house where He is staying, arrest Him at gun point, and deport him. Greek media reports indicate government and church pressure provoked the police intervention.

WORLD TOUR 1985 – 1986

February-March, 1986 cont.:
During the following two weeks He visits or asks permission to visit 17 countries in Europe and the Americas. All of these countries either refuse to grant Him a visitor's visa or revoke His visa upon His arrival, and force Him to leave. Some refuse even landing permission for His plane.

March-June, 1986:

On March 19 He travels to Uruguay. On May 14th the government has scheduled a press conference to announce that He will be granted permanent residence in Uruguay. Uruguay's President Sanguinetti later admits that he received a telephone call from Washington, D.C. the night before the press conference. He is told that if Osho is allowed to stay in Uruguay, the six billion dollar debt Uruguay owes to the United States will be due immediately and no further loans will be granted. Osho is ordered to leave Uruguay on June 18th.

WORLD TOUR 1985 – 1986

June-July, 1986:

During the next month He is deported from both Jamaica and Portugal. In all, 21 countries had denied Him entry or deported Him after arrival. On July 29, 1986, He returns to Mumbai, India.

July 1988:

Osho begins, for the first time in 14 years, to personally lead the meditation at the end of each evening's discourse. He also introduces a revolutionary new meditation technique called The Mystic Rose.

January 1987:

He returns to the ashram in Pune, India, which is renamed Rajneeshdham.

OSHO COMMUNE INTERNATIONAL 1987 – 1989

January-February 1989:

He stops using the name "Bhagwan," retaining only the name Rajneesh. However, His disciples ask to call Him 'Osho' and He accepts this form of address. Osho explains that His name is derived from William James' word 'oceanic' which means dissolving into the ocean. Oceanic describes the experience, He says, but what about the experiencer? For that we use the word 'Osho.' At the same time, He came to find out that 'Osho' has also been used historically in the Far East, meaning "The Blessed One, on Whom the Sky Showers Flowers."

The Life of Osho | A Timeline

March-June 1989:
Osho is resting to recover from the effects of the poisoning, which by now are strongly influencing His health.

July 1989:
His health is getting better and He makes two appearances for silent darshans during the Festival, now renamed Osho Full Moon Celebration.

OSHO COMMUNE INTERNATIONAL 1987 – 1989

August 1989:
Osho begins to make daily appearances in Gautama the Buddha Auditorium for evening darshan. He inaugurates a special group of white-robed sannyasins called the "Osho White Robe Brotherhood." All sannyasins and non-sannyasins attending the evening darshans are asked to wear white robes.

September 1989:
Osho drops the name "Rajneesh," signifying His complete discontinuity from the past. He is known simply as "Osho," and the ashram is renamed "Osho Commune International."

January 1990:

During the second week in January, Osho's body becomes noticeably weaker. On January 18, He is so physically weak that He is unable to come to Gautama the Buddha Auditorium. On January 19, His pulse becomes irregular. When His doctor inquires whether they should prepare for cardiac resuscitation, Osho says, "No, just let me go. Existence decides its timing." He leaves His body at 5 p.m.

OSHO LEAVES HIS BODY 1990

January 1990 cont:

At 7 p.m. His body is brought to Gautama the Buddha Auditorium for a celebration, and is then carried to the burning ghats for cremation. Two days later, His ashes are brought to Osho Commune International and placed in His samadhi in Chuang Tzu Auditorium with the inscription:

OSHO
Never Born
Never Died
Only Visited This Planet Earth Between
11 December 1931 – 19 January 1990

Coming Soon from Sammasati publishing

Notes Written on My Heart
by Anando

Also in preparation:
Osho, Messiah of Life, Love and Laughter
by Swami Devageet

For more information on Osho visit:
Osho.com
Oshoheritagetrust.org
Oshoviha.org

Osho's active meditations, music and talks
available through:
newearthrecords.com

Sammasati
publishing

Sammasati means:

"Right Remembrance"
The mind is utterly empty, and you are simply there in that emptiness. A kind of presence, a pure presence, with nowhere to go — utterly relaxed into oneself, at rest, at home. That is the meaning of Buddha's meditation.

~Osho